# A WORLD EVENT

Though the TATTOOS book, and the "Antidote For Addiction" 30 Days To Life Deliverance Program were conceived, written, and first offered within the walls of a Federal Prison, God's Plan is for them are much bigger than that. He desires they be offered to a world audience!

You do not have to be in, have been in, or actually go to a physical prison of any kind to reap the rewards of the Deliverance from Addiction shared within these materials. The many facets of the Prison of Addiction are more than enough to meet the need for such a *Deliverance* message.

Addiction has reared its ugly head up in every arena of life and has not and will not discriminate, in any fashion to continue reeking its havoc upon humankind.

No matter where you find yourself, or that of a loved one, the "Antidote For Addiction" is waiting to be discovered.

May God's Peace Guide your walk in and through it as you strive to experience Deliverance.

## ADDICTION CONNECTION DISCLAIMER:

The journey in this 30 Days To Life Program and the story in the TATTOOS book are NOT intended to imply that there is a correlation between Tattoos and Substance Abuse Addiction or Addiction of Any Kind. It is the telling of Cody's Journey in recognizing his addictive tenancies. He reveals where he was physically, relationally, emotionally, and spiritually throughout the journey of his Tattoos. He does this with the hope of helping others, quite possibly yourself or a loved one, find not only the beginning, but the middle, and most importantly, the end to the most personal debilitating addictions. He has gone on to create this 30 Days to Life *Deliverance* Program to allow addicts and their loved ones to see and engage exactly how the "Antidote For Addiction", Spiritually Graced Forgiveness may work in their lives. Once again, with the hope and belief that one day soon you will hear from your own lips or from those of a loved one, the same truth that came from Cody's, "I am *Delivered* from my Addiction."

## ADDICTION RECOVERY DISCLAIMER:

The publishing of the "30 Days To Life *Deliverance* Program" is NOT intended to be a stand in for, or a replacement of the addiction recovery programs and services offered by professionals in that field. Our hope is that it will serve, where called, as a powerful prerequisite for and/or addition to those very programs. We will trust God to guide you in your direction for and choice of recovery programs.

PriscillAquila Press 2022

# ANTIDOTE FOR ADDICTION
## 30 DAYS TO LIFE

## *Deliverance*

### CODY LANUS
#### WITH GARY MARTEL

## PROGRAM
## SURVIVING THE PERFECT STORM OF ADDICTION

***Antidote for Addiction***
*30-Days to Life Deliverance Program*
Copyright @2022 by Cody Lanus with Gary Martel

All rights reserved. No part of this book may be reproduced in any manner whatsoever without the expressed written permission of the author.

Published by:
PriscillAquila Press
288 Deerfield Estates Rd.
Boone, NC 28607

Print ISBN: 978-1-7370033-0-4
eBook ISBN: 978-1-7370033-3-5

Editors: GJ Martel / ES Parker / JO Saladino

Cover & Interior Design: Fusion Creative Works

Printed in the United States of America

To Jesus Christ:

Our Lord, Savior, Deliverer,

Source of Inspiration and Strength

&

To all those who have yet to embrace

*Deliverance*, this Program is for you.

## Praise, Endorsements, and Testimonies for
# "TATTOOS" &
# "ANTIDOTE FOR ADDICTION"

"I've attended Cody's 30DTL Ministry in Federal Prison. I've been to other treatment programs and it's a breath of fresh air for someone to finally give Jesus Christ the credit He deserves for Delivering us. Praise God! A book and program finally arrive to give Glory to what Jesus Christ has already done on the cross! As a black man, it was wonderful to see all races, cultures and ethnicities come together in Federal Prison under one banner, Christianity."

-Dr. Ivan L. Robinson DNP

"Captivating and extremely hard to put down. These are the best ways to describe "Tattoos." With many distractions in prison, it says volumes about a book that grabs your attention and has you wanting to read it all the way through. Being in and out of the troughs of addiction for over 10 years, I have been subject to many types of treatment. But when I got to FPC Butner and met Cody, to see the passion he has for the Lord and to help others was exhilarating. I have believed in God my entire life and through other programs He has always been my "Higher Power", but to see a program and the creator of the program give all the glory to God was that one final piece I was missing in my journey to help solidify my recovery. I will forever be grateful for meeting Cody Lanus and having the pleasure of reading his book and being a part of his 30DTL program here in prison. The Hope I have seen this program bring to prisoners in a place where there isn't much of it, is nothing short of amazing. I know many, many more people will soon be impacted just as I was. God bless."

-Brad Scott Bruce Jr.

"Cody's Faith driven reform should be a catalyst of recovery for those ready for change. "TATTOOS, My Gateway Drug" will provide just that. A must read!"

-Randall S. King Author of "The Color of Hate"

"Being educated, diverse, and well-established through my works, I never thought I'd ever come to prison. The reality of God's plan for me to spend time here made me question my very desire to live. The 30-Day To Life Deliverance Program30DTL, from Day 1 inspired me to refocus and to find a peace in my suffering and purpose and in my service to God. I've learned to stand on God's Word while carrying my cross daily. Cody Lanus is an exceptional man. His stewardship, honor and innate leadership draws everyone close to the God we serve. I thank God for the 30DTL Program, and I thank God for the "Antidote to my Addiction."

-L. Jarman, Butner Inmate

"To Cody's Reading Audience: I write this testament for Cody without reservation. I further attest to knowing Cody for over 3 years while incarcerated with him. It's my privilege to know and interact with Cody as a fellow Christian brother, as a man, despite of this caustic and negative arena we find ourselves in. Certain men, woman, and children possess the "It" factor that separates them as very special, gifted and blessed individuals. Cody has "It" immediately upon meeting him. The "It" factor is set aside by Cody though. I find that people like Cody play a massive role in this society and world. His humility is beyond measurable. Cody is filled with an inner light and peace that eludes his outer self. It has a lot to do with his sincerity, joyfulness, peacefulness and most dramatically, his faith in Christ."

-R. P. L Fellow Christian Brother in Christ

"This is a special book that follows the slide from high school and collegiate sports success to arrival at Federal Prison on drug charges. The highlight of the book is Cody's fight to regain his balance through growth in God. His positive attitude and prescriptions for rebuilding a shattered life should be an example to all of us."

-Terry Smith, Ph.D.

# CONTENTS

| | | |
|---|---|---|
| Day 1 | Forward, Preface, Prologue | 21 |
| Day 2 | Chapter 1: The Spiraling/Inward, Outward | 29 |
| Day 3 | Chapter 1: The Spiraling/Downward, Too Much | 35 |
| Day 4 | Chapter 2: Innocent Beginnings | 41 |
| Day 5 | Chapter 3: Empower Me? | 47 |
| Day 6 | Chapter 4: The Creep of Darkness | 55 |
| Day 7 | Chapter 5: The First Taste Of Addiction's Link | 63 |
| Day 8 | Chapter 6: The Executioner's Portal… Inward/Outward | 67 |
| Day 9 | Chapter 6: The Executioner's Portal… Downward/Too Far I Go! | 71 |
| Day 10 | Chapter 7: The Executioner's Voice… Too Much/Too Deep/Too Far, Again! | 77 |
| Day 11 | Chapter 8: The Search For Equilibrium… With-in The Family/ With-in The Coaches | 87 |
| Day 12 | Chapter 8: The Search For Equilibrium… With-in Myself/ With-in the Weights | 93 |
| Day 13 | Chapter 9: The Deeper Darker State of Mind… Lessness /…Games | 97 |
| Day 14 | Chapter 10: The Cards Tumble… With Release/With Relief/With Pain | 111 |
| Day 15 | Chapter 11: 'County' A Taste Of Freedom | 119 |
| Day 16 | Chapter 12: 'Federal' A Taste Of Direction | 127 |

| | |
|---|---|
| Day 17 Chapter 13: The Story Of The Rose/ Begins in Confrontation | 133 |
| Day 18 Chapter 13: The Story Of The Rose/ Yet Progresses | 141 |
| Day 19 Chapter 14: The Calling… | 147 |
| Day 20 Chapter 15: The Logan Effect/Coincidence… | 155 |
| Day 21 Chapter 15: The Logan Effect/…Or Godscidence | 161 |
| Day 22 Chapter 16: Personalized Forgiveness/… 'To' Me | 173 |
| Day 23 Chapter 16: Personalized Forgiveness/ … 'To' Me (cont.) | 179 |
| Day 24 Chapter 16: Personalized Forgiveness/… 'From' Me. | 185 |
| Day 25 Chapter 16: Personalized Forgiveness/ … 'From' Me. (cont.) | 191 |
| Day 26 Chapter 17: The New Antidote/ Recognition, Injection, Liberation | 195 |
| Day 27 Epilogue: The Lasting Narcan | 203 |
| Day 28 Afterward/The Old Man's Words Of Encouragement | 217 |
| Day 29 Congratulations! | 235 |
| Day 30 What's Next?/Your Story Now Into Life | 241 |
| Additional Notes | 251 |
| About the Author/Creator | 263 |
| About the Collaborator | 265 |
| Bibliography | 267 |
| Additional Resources | 269 |

## *Deliverance:*

Being freed, liberated, and forgiven from the debt of your sin (addiction)…

# INTRODUCTION

The purpose of this program is to bring to life the reading of "TATTOOS, My Gateway Drug, Surviving The Perfect Storm Of Addiction."

My hope for this curriculum, is that it can further assist those struggling with addiction, beyond what the book alone can do in and of itself.

By providing a means to actually capture the thoughts of those who read the book, the reader who wants more will then be able to begin their own journey of healing, just as I did.

Additionally, challenging that very reader, hopefully you, to comprehensively navigate through their own experiences, I believe, allows for internal growth that reading alone cannot offer.

This 30 Days To Life *Deliverance* Program is that very blueprint.

Like the reading of the book, working your way through the program will not always be comfortable. As I wrote the book, I myself found that my emotions were sometimes hard to handle and hard to hide. I'm sure the same will occur within you as you continue through this program. This, I believe, would most likely not be possible for its fullest potential had you not taken the bold action to begin the program. I commend you for taking the first step, which is wanting change!

Now, change can be a challenging beast. I had a difficult time wrestling with the *New Man* that I became after being *Delivered* from my addictions. Furthermore, being incarcerated made those adjustments that much more difficult. There is a certain stigma, if you will, that incarcerated men and women are often supposed to accept, which had I allowed, would have greatly hindered the change I was seeking. Regardless of the stigma you may feel called to accept in your addiction, showing people the person, you want to be, is sometimes the hardest thing about changing in the first place. I think the Apostle Paul said it best in Romans 12:2 "And do not be conformed to this world, but be transformed by the renewing of your mind, that you may prove what is that good, acceptable and perfect will of God." Paul couldn't have said it any better. I myself was sure tired of being conformed to the wrong things. I trust you can relate to what I speak.

But there are many other factors, other than wanting to change, that have led you to be working through this program. I am not a doctor, so let me be clear that my intentions are not to cure, treat, prevent, or diagnose any individual that is reading the book or working this program. Yet, my goal is to lead you to discover *The One* that can.

This is not a 12-step program, AA, NA, or rehab. Think of this program as a tool to assist in helping you recognize and understand the voids in your life that played a part in leading to your addiction. Identifying the voids, and what surrounds them that led you to begin taking mind altering substances to fill them in the first place. Then, I believe that you can lay a solid foundation for understanding *who* it is that you need in applying the core theme of the book. What is the core theme of the book you ask? The core theme is the "Antidote for Addiction." As you work through the book and the program, you will discover *who* and *what Delivered* me from my addictions. You will discover the "Antidote for Addiction" yourself.

Being *Delivered* is much different than any typical program used for those struggling with addictions to drugs or alcohol. Being *Delivered* means that you no longer have the stigma to identify yourself as being an "addict" or an "alcoholic." Being *Delivered* means that you no longer have to carry those mental, stressful, and spiritual burdens everywhere you go in life, because I believe at that moment you are anything but an addict, and so does He!

I also believe that the burdens we carried, the same burdens that led to our addictions to drugs and alcohol, are much greater than any human is capable of carrying alone and surviving the storm unscathed. This is why we found drugs and alcohol to be so addictive, for a moment they help us forget.

This trauma that led us to begin and remain for a difficult season in bondage to our addictions, can only be made free by the Healing Power of God, yes, God!

Furthermore, discovering who the *mediator* is between God and us, along with what He did for us to be free from such bondage, allows you to understand why it is no longer acceptable to remain labeled as such a degrading name like "addict" or "alcoholic." You are much greater than those words.

All of the things that I've just mentioned are Key Principals for the 30 Days To Life Deliverance Program that lies before you: wanting change, understanding your voids, identifying what you need to effectively apply the Antidote for Addiction, recognizing your inability to carry burdens alone, and understanding what God has done in your life so that you no longer have to carry those burdens.

By allowing yourself to embrace this program, and understanding those Key Principals, it is my whole-hearted belief that you will recognize just how important you are and just how much you are loved. This is the very *Deliverance* that I speak of. Trust me, from that position, the last thing you'll ever want to do again is use drugs and alcohol.

So, please move forward with an open mind, an open heart, and the open invitation for Spiritual growth. I encourage you to have a Bible to accompany you as soon as possible. Though there are many translations, we use the New King James Version (NKJV) throughout this program. It will be easier for you to not let a different translation be a stumbling block during this time, as their will be challenges enough along the way. My recommendation is to wait until after the program to explore other Bible versions. This is not a hard and fast requirement to proceed, as it will ultimately be the Holy Spirit who will be bringing you understanding and bringing Him alive in you.

Also, you will find a personal journal to be most helpful in keeping your journey's thoughts, expressions, and extension to questions you will be asked throughout. Begin today.

# INTRODUCTION

If you pray, I encourage you to pray before beginning each lesson, and if you don't, I encourage you to close your eyes and simply meditate on what it is you want to accomplish each day. Or, if you'd like, you can simply refer to this simple prayer before beginning each lesson every single day:

*"Dear Lord, I enter this prayer in the name of your Son Jesus Christ. I pray for Wisdom, and Knowledge as I continue forward on today's lesson. I pray that you allow my mind and heart to be open, and for the Holy Spirit to move me mightily. Most importantly, I acknowledge and accept that Jesus Christ is my personal Lord and Savior. I know that by saying this prayer, you will guide me to a life free from addiction and/ or bondage of any kind. Father I am not an addict or an alcoholic but loved, by You. In Jesus' name, Amen."*

He has Great Faith in you, and so do I.

"Now may the God of hope fill you with all joy and peace in believing, that you may abound in hope by the power of the Holy Spirit." Romans 15:13

God bless you as you move forward,

Cody Lanus

# DAY 1

## FOREWORD, PREFACE AND PROLOGUE

**FORWARD:**

In the Foreword of TATTOOS, on pages 11 and 12, Ellen Smith Parker says, "This story allows healing and shows where we get the restorative power. Hebrews 11:1 to me says 'faith is being sure of what we hope for, and certain of what we do not see.' Regardless of your level of faith, or your understanding of it, this book is bound to increase the faith within you."

*Deliverance* from drugs or alcohol is not a tangible thing, meaning we can't reach out and touch it. Therefore, one of the most pivotal aspects of deliverance is faith. For you to be reading these words, you evidently possess some level of faith in what I'm saying. You have read of my deliverance from drug addiction by the healing power of Jesus Christ. Therefore, by continuing to read my words you surely possess, possibly unknowingly, the same measure of faith that I found I had for Jesus, to now deliver you from your addiction.

Paul, the writer of Hebrews goes into great detail about how there are many people in history that have done some pretty amazing things by simply having faith that He would deliver them from their plight as well. You too, have access to His amazing healing power. How? By simply beginning with a small measure of faith.

Now use that small measure of faith and say this Powerful Prayer:

*"Dear Lord, I enter this prayer in the name of your son Jesus Christ. I pray for faith as I continue through this 30-day program. I know that I will need faith to continue forward, as I'm seeking something that sometimes feels impossible to conquer. By trusting You, I know that anything is possible. Even the deliverance from drugs and alcohol. Your word says, "For by Grace you have been saved through faith." Father, I believe that by my faith in You, You will deliver me. In Jesus Christ's name, Amen."*

A major part of the "Antidote of Addiction" is forgiveness. There is much to this unique forgiveness, as you will surely discover as you continue your journey through this 30-day program. However, grasping the fundamentals of forgiveness is particularly important. Ellen tells us that the dictionary definition of forgiveness is "The action or process of forgiving or being forgiven-release of debt." We all have our own ideas and concepts of forgiveness shaped throughout our lives. Some may be good, and some, not so much.

On page 13 Ellen goes on to say, "Cody has been able to gain strength from the writing process himself and shared the antidote of how we can lessen pain through forgiveness of ourselves and of others and arrive at peace." Your writing is about to begin.

Pause now, and write out your current personal definition of forgiveness:

_____

_____

_____

You have completed your first task. Way to go!

There it is! On page 13 Ellen mentions the word "antidote." The very thing you will discover that released me from my addiction! Currently, your thought of an antidote to lessen the pain when it comes, is by using drugs and/or alcohol. However, if you're anything like I was, you know that when the high wears off, the pain comes back as quickly as it left.

In this section, I want to pose a very difficult question that is paramount in traveling on your journey. A question that I was frequently presented with from Gary, The Old Man you will soon become familiar with, or be reminded of as you move forward.

Pause now. I would like you to give your best attempt at answering the very difficult question:

Why did you begin using drugs and/or alcohol? (For now, your best real deep why, the one that was the *pain* you felt you were living with, or the *void* in your life you were working to fill.)

_____
_____
_____
_____
_____
_____
_____
_____

As challenging as that was, you are setting a pattern for the direction of your journey. Nice job!

## PREFACE:

In the Preface, I ask the reader to look back at the events that led this book to be in their possession. Here is an opportunity to actually answer that very question.

Below, identify three reasons why you chose to read the "TATTOOS" book and engage in this "ANTIDOTE FOR ADDICTION" program. There are no right or wrong answers, and they can vary from, "A family member gave it/referred it to me," all the way to "I was court ordered to complete some type of addiction program" . Ok, now pause, ponder, and write.

1. _____
2. _____
3. _____

Your journey builds. There you go!

1 Corinthians 13:13 says "And now abide faith, hope, love, these three, but the greatest of these is love."

A major component of being *Delivered*, is learning to love yourself as you are "In Christ." We will go into this in greater detail throughout the program. But for now, I'd like you to identify three positive characteristics about yourself. Maybe you like your hair, or maybe others have told you that you are a good listener. Those are the types of things you are identifying here. Remember, there is no right or wrong answers.

1. _____
2. _____
3. _____

Your journey continues!

## PROLOGUE:

On page 21 Cody opens with, "They didn't cuff him. They didn't need to. To him, he'd been rescued. Something he saw no need in fleeing from. He didn't need to guess anymore. Death or Prison? He knew which one he'd reached. A Tupac song he'd willed into existence. 'His' existence. For him, you could have put the Federal Agents up there with the Narcan that had previously brought him back to life, Guardian Angels. He didn't want to hurt them he wanted to hug them."

Now, you also may be in a position in which you believe, as I once did that "Death or Prison" are the only options available for the outcome of you actually "quitting" the use of drugs/alcohol. The good thing is that you're here in search of the possibility of a third option. You are participating in this program in the hopes of discovering it for yourself. Our prayer is that you never encounter either one of the first two, but that you will discover and embrace the third.

As you just read, I once related my life to a Tupac song that I seemed to will into existence for my life. A "Thug Life" of sorts for me. This type of willing happens to many of us. Music for me has always been a sort of escape if you will. You can possibly relate in some way. The challenge in this next exercise is to find a song, a story, or a quote that relates to you or your life that you may soon recognize you willed into existence.

1. Write down some, or all of the lyrics, story or quote.

_____
_____
_____

2. What about these words speak to you?

_____
_____
_____

As you read the Prologue and continue through both the book and program, you may also be fearing the possible uncomfortable feelings of withdrawal, just as I did when the DEA agents finally arrested me in the story of the Prologue. You may have already felt these very feelings of withdrawal I speak of. Withdrawal, or being "Dopesick", can be a driving fear as to why people continue to make the decision to use drugs or alcohol. This is a lie we often tell ourselves. In fulfilling your plan of quitting drugs or alcohol, it is important that you monitor any feelings of discomfort or distress as you continue forward.

Pause for a moment and write down any current fears you may be encountering. This will assist you in looking back and seeing them as a lie as you continue your journey.

_____
_____
_____
_____
_____
_____

Way to go my friend! It can be scary, but you will find it worth the exposure.

Now, I encourage you to say this prayer and I call upon you to refer to it any time you feel it necessary.

*"Dear Lord, I enter this prayer in the name of your Son Jesus Christ. Father, Your Word says that "I can do all things through Christ who strengthens me." I pray for Your strength as I continue through this 30-day program. Lord, I ask for this strength as these toxins exit my body. Guide me, lead me, and direct me through this difficult time. I pray for motivation and healing Father. I entrust this detoxification process to Your hands. In Jesus Christ's name, Amen.*

Congratulations! You have completed Day 1 of the 30-day program.

I am proud of you. Let this all sink in for at least 24 hours before you continue. Please be sure to review the questions, callings, encouragements, and prayers offered in this day, before you start on the next new day.

Trust that you will become settled within this journey.

Gods got you. He believes in you and so do I.

# DAY 2

## CHAPTER 1

Welcome back. Let's open the day up with this Powerful Petition with Thanksgiving Prayer: (Taking the lead from Philippians 4:6,7)

*"Dear Lord, I enter this prayer in the name of Your son Jesus Christ. I pray and thank You for allowing my faith in You to come alive in me as I continue through this 30-day program. I know that it is by faith that I continue forward, as I'm seeking something that sometimes feels impossible to conquer. By trusting You, I know that anything is possible including faith in being delivered from drugs and alcohol. Your word says, "For by Grace you have been saved through faith." Father, I believe that by my faith in You, You will deliver me. In Jesus Christ's name, Amen."*

I trust that you have completed and reviewed your answers from Day 1, setting the stage for today. Let's continue in Chapter 1.

### THE SPIRALING …INWARD:

1. It seems I've always had an uncanny ability to manipulate people or situations to benefit me. On page 27, I talk about bending rules to fit my will. At first, like the rules I speak of, they seem miniscule. However, over time, the rules being bent were much

more serious. It can be said, especially regarding those who struggle with drugs and alcohol, that most of us have no idea how we have allowed our addictions to control our lives. Take a moment, close your eyes, and think about some situations you feel that you've "bent to your will" to get something you've wanted.
Now pause and write out the one or two that came to mind.

1. _____
   _____

2. _____
   _____

Way to go. It is not always easy to look back at these things as they are exposed, but we assure you it is well worth it as part of your journey.

2. "For God so loved the world that He gave His only begotten Son, that whoever believes in Him should not perish but have everlasting life." John 3:16

On page 30 I mention not having high self-esteem. Though it was a well-kept secret and others might never have guessed, it was true. As you read and re-read through the book, you recognize this to be a common theme and a contributing factor in my drug use. When I finally understood my position "In Christ," and what He did for me on the cross, I understood how important I actually was to Him. To acknowledge that God sent His Son to die for us, was to know a love I never fully understood before. This famous scripture from Jesus, in the Gospel of John, tells us of this love.

Pause and take a moment to think of some people you have an immense amount of love for, just as God does for you. These can be parents, spouses, children, close friends, etc.

1. _____
2. _____
3. _____
4. _____

Then, write down some people you believe to have this same immense amount of love for you.

1. _____
2. _____
3. _____
4. _____ and more!

If this brought up some tears, anger, or angst that's ok. It is all part of the journey of deliverance. Proud of you.

## ...OUTWARD:

On page 34, I mention participating in prayers at work in order to maintain an "outwardly Christian appearance." I had no prayer life outside of my work obligations at Boys Town. You may be able to relate, as might many other "Christians" if they were to speak truthfully. As I grew in my faith, I learned that setting aside time for quiet meditation along with conversational prayer was crucial in my fellowship and my growing relationship with God.

Choose and schedule a suitable time in your day, each and every day for prayer?

_____ (Monday-Friday)

_____ (Saturday, Sunday)

This should be a time with minimal or no outside distractions. I would encourage beginning with no less than 10 minutes, with the goal of increasing over time as you develop a deeper relationship with God.

On page 37 I mention the bumper sticker "WWJD?" ("<u>W</u>hat <u>W</u>ould Jesus <u>D</u>o?"). It's a popular acronym that's been asked frequently by many Christians in the face of any roadblock (i.e., an adversity, challenge, hardship). Yet, back in the car that day, you saw how I allowed a (deceptive) voice in me to manipulate and appease my mind, allowing it to work for me. Clearly, you have already deduced that it was not, and is not the intention of, or best use of "WWJD?" Amazing is the power of that self-deception, which you will discover more about on this journey!

Well, today I often present myself with the "WWJD" question as it was correctly meant to be asked and answered. I no longer ask myself "What would Jesus do?" Instead, I ask the One who holds the best answer, God. Yes, as a prayer to Him, I ask, "What would Jesus Call Me To Do?" Then as I listen, in time the "Guiding" answer comes. You will find this especially powerful for you to engage throughout your life when you come across *any* difficult situation.

# DAY 2

Pause and identify a major roadblock in your life and write it down. For this exercise begin with just one for now. You will have ample opportunity to add more later.

1. _____
   _____
   _____
   _____

Now, before you get to asking, and waiting for the answer to, "What Would Jesus Call Me To Do?" start by asking yourself and answering, "What would I do on my own?" Or if it was a previous roadblock, write out the answer to, "How have I handled this roadblock in the past?"

2. _____
   _____
   _____
   _____

You just created a reference point for you to begin to see the difference between your intellectually reasoned answer, like the one I created when I saw that bumper sticker, and His Spiritually Graced answer. With that in mind, take a few moments to rephrase the question to God in a conversational prayer, "Ok God, what would Jesus have me do with this roadblock?" Write out a prayer below and include the actual wording of the roadblock itself inside the prayer.

3. _____
   _____
   _____
   _____

Wow! You have done a great job engaging today. Now finish the day with the commitment to have your ears open to His voice to hear His answer for your question. We don't always receive instant answers though be assured He already knows. Wait on His clear word. Then, write it down when it comes.

4. _____
_____
_____
_____

You will grow mightily as you begin to see the difference between the two answers.

Be sure to read the rest of Chapter 1 and I will see you soon when you enter Day 3.

# DAY 3

## CHAPTER 1

Welcome back. Keep your faith alive as we travel through the rest of Chapter 1. Remember God is already working in you so be sure to open up with your daily Petition Prayer <u>with Thanksgiving</u>:

*"Dear Lord, I enter this prayer in the name of Your son Jesus Christ. I pray and thank You for allowing my faith in You to come alive in me as I continue through this 30-day program. I know that it is by faith that I continue forward, as I'm seeking something that sometimes feels impossible to conquer. By trusting You, I know that anything is possible including faith in being delivered from drugs and alcohol. Your word says, "For by Grace you have been saved through faith." Father, I believe that by my faith in You, You will deliver me. In Jesus Christ's name, Amen."*

Now that you are reminded that you are fully armed, let's move with Cody from Inward and Outward and look at …

## THE SPIRALING ...DOWNWARD:

1. On page 40, I reference a "voice" that I began hearing as I repeatedly made poor decisions. It wasn't a voice I constantly heard per se, but rather a growing intuition that nudged me to take the road that

would lead to my eventual incarceration. My intuitions or thoughts somehow convinced me that risky decisions, weren't so risky, allowing me to be okay making them. Can you relate? My experience tells me that you can. Now, write out a situation in which you know you justified partaking in risky behavior which was led by the same intuition or thoughts.

_____
_____
_____
_____
_____

Way to dig deep. Keep this memory in mind as you continue.

2. On page 42, I mention living a "life nobody seemed to suspect." A Jekyll and Hyde life, a double life. I was a youth care supervisor that regularly used drugs. Looking back now, it's hard to see how I pulled it off. But then again, because of my growing ability to manipulate people, I was good at leading them to believe I was just fine. (Including believing it myself!)

The truth is, I was far from it. Most, possibly you as well, while struggling in addiction, were very good at hiding it. The truth is that nothing in addiction can truly be hidden.

Hebrews 4:13 says:

"And there is no creature hidden from His sight, but all things are naked and open to the eyes of Him to whom we must give account."

Pause for a moment to ponder this, then write a short note or letter to someone you've always wanted to admit to or share your addiction struggles with.

_____
_____
_____
_____
_____

Breathe my friend. You do not have to send the note/letter in order for it to have its initial impact on you. I sense you already feel a bit of Spiritual Release is at hand. Rest with that for now.

3. On page 43, I mention seeing "a picture of Jesus wearing a crown of thorns. He met Jesus' eyes and for a moment they stared at each other. Jesus…a head tilted and a desperate (*almost sad*) look on his face."

How I imagined His pain was not from carrying the cross but from what He saw as He looked at me, the willful and self-centered Cody making the decisions I was making and living the life I was living. Imagine, here was Jesus, The Son of God, bearing the sins of man for all eternity on the cross, yet I was breaking His heart by my willingly using and selling drugs!

It was that glimpse of the "Truth" that overwhelmingly confronted me that day. We have all had those "Come to see Jesus!" moments, and on this particular day, this was one of mine. Then, I chose to follow the other voice in me which made it ok to not surrender just yet. For me to turn away in an instant and to re-engage life on my terms. Jesus would have to wait a little bit longer.

Surely you have had your own "Come to see Jesus!" moments throughout your time of addiction. Only to turn in an instant back to life on your terms.

Stop right here and write out what event has come to your mind that seems a parallel event to mine. Be bold, be brave, and lay it out.

_____

_____

_____

_____

Good job! Let's keep the flow going by revisiting a time of late that you were conceivably able to surrender all. When you actually went from those "Come to see Jesus!" moments to an actual "Coming to Jesus!" moment.*

Take a moment and write about this Powerful Event. How it has impacted your life so far. How you feel by surrendering and "Coming To Jesus." How it has helped you grow.

_____

_____

_____

_____

*If you feel this has not happened for you yet, keep moving, keep engaging, keep believing, keep the faith, keep praying the prayers, and your time will come.

Once again, way to go. So proud of you for staying personally engaged! Now, let's venture into the most challenging frontier in addiction.

## ...TOO MUCH:

4. You will find that on page 48 it reads, "Cody's thoughts of a purer life only existed within the hours spent behind a steering wheel. These car talks he'd frequently have with himself and God while driving were the only real words with substance and truth he was having in his life."

You see that my car was my church, in a sense. However, just as I outline in the book, the moment I stepped out of my vehicle, all of my talks with God were thrown to the wind, forgotten. Maybe you have a place you frequently find yourself talking to someone, or God. A place you might call your *church* where you pray to or have a conversation with God. It seems we share something in common with each other and Jesus in that respect. Scripture tells us that Jesus prayed to His Father and in many cases, He went out somewhere to do so.

The Apostle John reminds us that no matter what we ask, if we do so in the name of Jesus Christ, He will do it in a way that He may be glorified:

"Most assuredly, I say to you, he who believes in Me, the works that I do he will do also; and greater works than these he will do, because I go to My Father. And whatever you ask in My name, that I will do, that the Father may be glorified in the Son. If you ask anything in My name, I will do it." John 14:12-14

On a separate piece of paper, write out the above scripture. Then place it in your *church* where you often find yourself having a conversation with God. It could be your car, bedroom, bathroom, or place of work. Read it when you feel like you are not being listened to, as a reminder to yourself that in fact, you are always heard. God misses nothing and responds mightily to those words you speak in His Son's Name.

Well done for today my friend. Let it all sink in. You are doing an amazing job. When you are ready, read Chapter 2 and we will see you when you engage Day 4. May Jesus continue to bless you as you continue on your journey.

# DAY 4

## CHAPTER 2

Welcome to Day 4. You are beginning to create the habit of revealing some truths of your season of addiction by honestly answering the questions and directives posed to you by Cody. This is what is making this Your Journey. Keep the good pace in this.

Also remember to keep your faith alive as well. Yes, God is already working in you so be sure to open up with your daily Petition prayer with thanksgiving:

*"Dear Lord, I enter this prayer in the name of Your son Jesus Christ. I pray and thank You for allowing my faith in You to come alive in me as I continue through this 30-day program. I know that it is by faith that I continue forward, as I'm seeking something that sometimes feels impossible to conquer. By trusting You, I know that anything is possible including faith in being delivered from drugs and alcohol. Your word says, "For by Grace you have been saved through faith." Father, I believe that by my faith in You, You will deliver me. In Jesus Christ's name, Amen."*

With the knowledge that you have made a great connection with God, let's visit some of Cody's beginnings and open up some of your own.

## INNOCENT BEGINNINGS

1. As you just re-read in the early part of Chapter 2, I spoke about the experience of going to get and choosing my first tattoo, the tribal sun placed on my back. It was an impactful time, forever imbedded in my mind. I trust that if you have a single tattoo or many, you have a first-time experience imbedded in you as well. Pause and think back on that day.

Now, describe the events going to get your first tattoo including the *emotions* you had during that time.

_____
_____
_____
_____
_____

Next, write out the reasons why you chose to get one. Think back on the real "Why?"

_____
_____
_____
_____

If you don't have a tattoo don't worry. Take a moment and write out why you decided to never get one.

_____
_____
_____
_____

"My Gateway Drug" was my tattoos. In them a pattern of behavior in addiction became obvious to me looking back, thus the revelation of the book in your hand. Yet not everyone who found themselves in the throes of addiction have a pattern of behavior that began with tattoos. As you open yourself up throughout this program, it is my hope that you will discover your "Gateway Drug." That thing in your life that in looking back you recognize was the very thing you leaned on or engaged in that started the behavior. When you discover it, take the time to write it out in the same fashion as I just asked above, describing that first day and the real "Why?"

_____
_____
_____
_____
_____
_____

2. On page 61, I talk about a *significant* life event: The divorce of my mother and stepfather. As I wrote the book, feelings of anger re-surfaced. They were feelings that had clearly laid dormant, some I was unaware even existed, albeit all leading to some of my addictions, as later I go on to describe. Does this begin to ring true for you as you read about it? Let the ringing continue as you stop for a bit. Listen and really ponder a *significant* life event (or a series of smaller related events) from your younger years. The one(s) that you feel have impacted you greatly, just as the divorce did for me.

Take your time, then write out in your words how you remembered it (them).

Remember to thank God in prayer for being on board with you here as He assists in absorbing the desire of the old ways of dealing with these possible triggering events.

_____
_____
_____
_____
_____
_____

3. At the end of page 62, I speak of my Spiritual Faith at the time of that tattooed summer as being "…iffy at best." I go on to say of my revelation of the time:

"There I was squeezing my hands to numb the pain of the needle driving ink below the surface of my skin. I did not know at the time the little grip I had with God was slipping," below the surface as well.

At this point in your 30-day to Life Program, take some time to describe how you feel your spiritual life is developing.

_____
_____
_____
_____
_____
_____

Wow! You really are growing in faith and making progress by this continued engagement. Though it may not be easy for you at times to dig deep, I sense you are understanding the power behind doing so.

I continue to be proud of you.

Now, let all of this day settle in and embrace all that has come to you. Then, read Chapter 3 and I will see you again when you enter Day 5.

# DAY 5

## CHAPTER 3

Welcome to Day 5. Nice job on your previous day's work. You are continuing to grow in your knowledge and understanding of your season in addiction.

Always remember to keep your faith alive as well. God is working in you as you open up with your daily Petition prayer with thanksgiving:

*"Dear Lord, I enter this prayer in the name of Your son Jesus Christ. I pray and thank You for allowing my faith in You to come alive in me as I continue through this 30-day program. I know that it is by faith that I continue forward, as I'm seeking something that sometimes feels impossible to conquer. By trusting You, I know that anything is possible including faith in being delivered from drugs and alcohol. Your word says, "For by Grace you have been saved through faith." Father, I believe that by my faith in You, You will deliver me. In Jesus Christ's name, Amen."*

I encourage you to take a few minutes and re-read Chapter 3 to get you in the proper mindset for this day. Okay, lets continue your journey of deliverance.

## EMPOWER ME?

1. On page 63, I say, "I began to chase the high of a rebellious nature despite those I felt I might be hurting."
Many that are struggling with addiction can relate to the enjoyment of rebelling against authority. For some, this may be the "high" they enjoyed, even before trying drugs or alcohol.

Describe a situation in which you "rebelled against authority."

_____
_____
_____
_____

Now, describe the emotions *while* participating in that activity.

_____
_____
_____
_____

Finish with describing the emotions you felt *after* participating in that activity.

_____
_____
_____
_____

Good job!

2. On page 64, I link "chasing the high of my rebellious nature" to "gaining attention and acceptance." Simply put, when I rebelled,

it got me noticed and gave me the feeling of being liked as other people saw it as cool. Tattoos got me attention, especially when I was younger. "The tattoos seemed the gateway to all the others. Sex, drugs, alcohol, and more."

Stop for a moment and take this opportunity to continue to expound on what you believe to be your 'Gateway Drug.' Do you have a greater understanding of the "Why?"

_____
_____
_____
_____
_____
_____
_____
_____
_____

3. "For by Grace you have been saved through Faith, and that not of yourselves, it is the gift of God, not of works, lest anyone should boast." Ephesians 2:8-9

On page 66, I speak of my decision to get the Chinese symbol for Faith tattooed on the back of my right arm at the triceps. I chose that particular tattoo because it just seemed cool at the time. Many like myself on their tattoo decision day never stop to consider, let alone fully understand what their belief in God is. Nor do they think on their faith in Jesus Christ if they have any at all. Therefore, God or Jesus' impact on their decision making never comes into play. Yet, the very impact of placing our faith in Jesus Christ begins the working of miracles of deliverance in one's life, including the life of those struggling with addictions. Like the verse above from Ephesians says, we can literally be saved. Saved from a current life of sin. Yes, even saved from the throes of addiction. Therefore, I would like to invite you to participate in this prayer of faith with me:

*"Dear God, I place my faith in You and Your Son Jesus Christ who died on the cross for me and my sins. Through this Grace, given to me by Faith, I believe You will deliver me from the bondages of addiction. Father, only You can break those chains. You are the Way maker and the Chain breaker. In Jesus Christ's name, Amen."*

Now, with that Faith, continue your Journey. Remember to not only read the scripture passages written here but open your Bible from time to time and read them from there as well.

4. "Be strong and of good courage, do not fear nor be afraid of them, for the Lord your God, He is the One who goes with you." Deuteronomy 31:6

At the same time of the Faith tattoo, I also decided the Chinese symbol for Courage on the other triceps would be a great idea. I wasn't exactly sure why I got those exact cool words other than they "… might soften the blow with my Christian mom." At that young age, I wasn't exactly sure what courage really meant to me, yet like most young adults, I did seem to think I was invincible. "What did I need courage for?" I'd often think to myself when others asked what the tattoo symbol meant. The truth is, most of us who don't think we need courage, are in fact the ones who need it the most. Only later in my life I learned that true lasting courage can only come from the indwelling of God's Holy Spirit who is given to us when we place our faith in Jesus Christ. This is the same courage that it takes to attack your addiction head on, face first. For you to even be reading this shows an immense amount of courage by your willingness to begin this process of healing and deliverance.

Pause now and take some time to identify three situations for which you need courage in the upcoming months.

1. _____
   _____
   _____

2. _____
   _____
   _____

3. _____
   _____
   _____

Pray with thanksgiving on these three situations the way I have shown you to pray. Know that God knows you so well that He is already at work in those areas for you. Isn't that just fantastic? Let's keep moving.

5. "But God, who is rich in mercy, because of His great love with which He loved us, even when we were dead in our trespasses (*addiction*), made us alive together with Christ...." Ephesians 2:4

On page 68 you will find me saying, "As I looked, I thought of my faith for the first time in a long time. Of my relationship and trust in God and His Mercy." When I wrote that for the story, I didn't fully understand God's Mercy for me. I did have an inclination that it was some kind of forgiveness. One dictionary definition of mercy is, "the outward manifestation of pity." Yet, according to the scripture written above, the meaning of the word actually goes much deeper than just forgiveness. It becomes the actual manifestation of just such a forgiveness. The actual coming alive of the results of being forgiven without deserving it!

At the end of Chapter 3, I equate the hard times I was facing, feeling I was experiencing a lack of mercy from God. The truth was the exact opposite, I was experiencing an abundance of His Mercy. Yet, I was unable to recognize *It* due to my understanding of Christ and my walk with Christ or better yet my lack of both.

It is important to recognize that even at our lowest moments, God is right there with us. Yes, with you and me! The first glimpse of dawn always seems to come right after the darkest part of night.

Have you ever felt like God's Mercy was lacking? \_\_\_\_Yes \_\_\_\_No

Have you ever expected Mercy only to then think things were actually getting worse? \_\_\_Yes \_\_\_\_No

Now, I am going to challenge you to identify three positive situations that you now recognize actually arose out of a seemingly dark time in your life.

The dark time?

_____
_____
_____

The three positive situations?

1. _____
   _____
   _____

2. _____
   _____
   _____

3. _____
   _____
   _____

Now, that was a challenging but important exercise. I continue to be proud of you for stepping up and doing the assignments. You are growing as you do. Way to go!

Be sure to read Chapter 4 prior to jumping into Day 6. We will see you there when you are ready.

# DAY 6

## CHAPTER 4

Here we go into Day 6. You are continuing to engage and grow day by day. Keep up the good work.

Remember to keep your faith alive as well, allowing the Good Lord to work in you. Open with your daily Petition Prayer with thanksgiving:

*"Dear Lord, I enter this prayer in the name of Your son Jesus Christ. I pray and thank You for allowing my faith in You to come alive in me as I continue through this 30-day program. I know that it is by faith that I continue forward, as I'm seeking something that sometimes feels impossible to conquer. By trusting You, I know that anything is possible including faith in being delivered from drugs and alcohol. Your word says, "For by Grace you have been saved through faith." Father, I believe that by my faith in You, You will deliver me. In Jesus Christ's name, Amen."*

I trust you have revisited Chapter 4 as the best way of grasping what you are about to experience today. Okay, lets continue your journey of deliverance.

## THE CREEP OF DARKNESS

1. "And do not be conformed to this world, but be transformed by the renewing of your mind, that you may prove what is that good and acceptable and perfect will of God." Roman 12:2
*"We don't realize that left unchecked we lose sight of the view that matters most, God's. We then find ourselves replacing it with our friends view of us."*

Listen my friend, *conforming* to the world doesn't happen overnight. It didn't happen to me or you overnight either. It comes in the form of a constant attack of questions and or statements (which are actually lies) that we allow to play within our minds. Those questions and lies are given to us by the adversary. "What does the world think of me? Am I acceptable enough?" These are just two examples I mention that were playing in my mind of page 69, but as you well know the list goes on and on!

As the title of the chapter suggests, these questions are in fact the "Creep of Darkness." This is one of the most powerful tools that Satan has, using the weakness of our flesh, to "conform us to this world," his world of thinking and believing, just as Romans 12 says.

So, how do we not allow ourselves to play into these thoughts? The only way to ensure we do not fall into the hands of "Darkness" is "to be transformed by the renewing of our minds," just as Paul says. Denying our flesh is never easy, however we must understand that the outcomes are never good if we do not do so. The Bible uses the term being "unfruitful" to describe such activity. Furthermore, the best way to become "fruitful" is by utilizing, practicing, and making a habit of three things:

1. Reading The Word (Bible Scripture)

2. Praying (Conversational Asking, Thanking, and Listening)

3. Fellowship with other Christians (One-One, Books, Music, etc.)

Pause right now and pick one of these to focus on:

1, 2, or 3? _____

Now answer these two questions:

1. How are you going to ensure that it gets added to your daily schedule?

_____
_____
_____

2. What will you have to sacrifice in order to make it fit?

_____
_____
_____

2. On page 70 I speak of my previous view of surrendering. "Cody Lanus does not surrender! He prevails!" It took me a long time to learn that there is really nothing I could do myself to truly beat my addictions and that there was no "prevailing" by my own power. I had to finally recognize and trust in Jesus Christ, that He died on the cross for *all* of my sins. This included my sin in addiction of which He paid that ultimate penalty on the cross, for me to be delivered and free from it. I had to allow Jesus to be my Lord by surrendering myself, just as I was in the middle of my addiction, to

Him to realize that He is Lord over my entire life. This is the absolute surrender that God is expecting if we ever hope to be delivered from our addictions. We must stop rationalizing and excusing our lack of submission to God. If we do not, then we allow our addictions to continue unabated. Rather, we must trust and obey Him by surrendering all to Him. Gary, The Old Man, once told me that he fought comparing surrendering to God as the same as surrendering to someone in the world. He was raised to believe that to surrender was to give up power, therefore his 'pride' would not allow him to surrender and show weakness! This for him, proved the same end result as it did for me, prison! Then, to discover that surrendering his worldly pride to God allowed him to gain God's Greater Power for his life was a game changer. This same revelation discovery came to me, and I now pass it on to you. I encourage you to get with God and embrace your own revelation discovery of it. Then, take the action that will change your life. He believes in you to do just that.

Because of our limited intellectual capacity for remembering what all our life sins are, you will find that surrendering is not a onetime thing either, it's a lifelong practice lived out until the day we meet Him. Remember this so that when you find yourself stuck, by your own strength in a new area, you can call it out for what it is, and surrender it. Be delivered anew in that area. My contention is that confessing it, is surrendering it to God who hears it through His Holy Spirit in you.

This is why 1 John 1:9 is so powerful for us:

"If we confess our sins, He is faithful and just to forgive us our sins and cleanse us from all unrighteousness."

I challenge you to take a few minutes and ruminate on what you just read and answer these questions:

Are you afraid to surrender to God? \_\_\_\_ Yes \_\_\_\_ No

1. If Yes, what does that fear look like, sound like, and or feel like? (be specific).

   _____
   _____
   _____

2. What could you lose by surrendering to God?

   _____
   _____
   _____

3. More importantly, what can you gain?

   _____
   _____
   _____

Now, I know that this was a challenging section, but I assure you that as you completed the exercise the Good Lord was working in you for a new perspective, His perspective for your life. I sense that you are already forming that new perspective, even if you may not be able to completely describe it yet. Keep at it as it becomes more evident and clearer in you.

3. On page 72 I mention, "I lived life in hyper speed and downers would become my drug of choice." As you read on, I perceived they had more than one purpose than to slow my mind so that I could

sleep. When I got to prison and my head began to clear, I finally gave myself time to begin reflecting on my life. I came to the grim realization that due to the speed at which I was living during those times, I had neglected many areas of my life including relationships. I had refused to slow down and "smell the roses" as they say. I believe this was a big part of why I fell in love with drugs like opioids. They seemed to allow me the peace I was always searching for without the responsibility of a relationship. Yet it was actually a lie. That peace was artificial, and in fact was a relationship in and of itself. A relationship with a drug or thing that could not love me back and not with a person or persons who could and would love me back! Wow!

The real Peace I needed was a true Peace that only Jesus Christ could provide, not drugs. This Peace you will understand, embrace, and live more and more as you continue on your journey.

For now, pause and take a moment to list some areas of your life you feel that you've neglected because you have refused to slow down.

_____

_____

_____

_____

Nice job. Way to think into this challenging exercise.

4. Please read page 73 where I discuss re-emerging *red flags*. You can see these would slowly begin to pop up in my life, danger warnings that I regularly ignored until I found myself in a prison cell. A major goal in this program is to show you the path of deliverance long before prison becomes a destination. If you find yourself already there, take heart, the deliverance and freedom which can be yours will have an even greater impact.

At this point in your 30-day program, stop and take the time to identify at least one *red flag* in your life. (work to have it be one you can use as an anchor example as you move forward)

_____
_____
_____

Now, Write out what you feel to be a consequence of continually ignoring it.

_____
_____
_____

Lastly, write out what is a step you're going to take to make sure it stops popping up?

_____
_____
_____

Wow! You continue to make me proud of your commitment to dig deep here. Keep it up. It is paying off in more ways than you can yet realize. Trust me.

5. 2 Corinthians 1:3,4 reads, "Blessed be the God and Father of our Lord Jesus Christ, the Father of mercies and God of *all* comfort, who comforts us in *all* tribulation, that we may be able to comfort those who are in any trouble, with the comfort with which ourselves are comforted by God."

Even though I continually mention the negative *voice* or "Creep of Darkness" as the chapter is titled, I also mention a "Voice of Reason" on page 75. I have discovered and embraced the fact that this *voice* is

God's voice, God's Holy Spirit voice who is always right there with me. My hope is that you are coming to the same realizations too. That He is always right there with you.

Knowing that God is with me gives me a comfort that cannot be explained in intellectual terms because it is a spiritual comfort. Yet you will know it as it continues to come over you. This is the same comfort I've relied on so much while being incarcerated. It's also the same comfort that you too can rely on in your times of despair. It's a comfort that outweighs any temporary comfort any drug or drink can give.

Let me ask you, "Has God spoken to you? \_\_\_\_ Yes \_\_\_\_ No, not yet.

If yes, what is He saying right now in your life?

_____
_____
_____

If no, then I encourage you to write out a prayer asking Him to come and allow you to hear His Voice for your life. Be sure to add a thank you in it for Him hearing your prayer. Remember He already knows what you are searching for and is already on it!

_____
_____
_____

Now, rest peacefully knowing you have poured yourself into today's work in this program.

Be sure to re-read Chapter 5 before entering Day 7 of your journey. See you soon.

# DAY 7

## CHAPTER 5

Welcome back to Day 7. I trust you are really beginning to feel that this program is impacting your mind, body, and spirit in a way it has never been impacted before. This is what you are meant to experience on the journey. Keep at it. The final payoff is big.

Begin again keeping your faith alive as well by allowing the Good Lord to work in you today. Open up with the Petition Prayer with thanksgiving:

*"Dear Lord, I enter this prayer in the name of Your son Jesus Christ. I pray and thank You for allowing my faith in You to come alive in me as I continue through this 30-day program. I know that it is by faith that I continue forward, as I'm seeking something that sometimes feels impossible to conquer. By trusting You, I know that anything is possible including faith in being delivered from drugs and alcohol. Your word says, "For by Grace you have been saved through faith." Father, I believe that by my faith in You, You will deliver me. In Jesus Christ's name, Amen."*

Having re-read Chapter 5 let us jump right in.

## THE FIRST TASTE OF ADDICTION'S LINK

1. At the beginning of Chapter 5, you're introduced to Coach Stirtz, my High School Basketball coach. As I mention, "The coach was the first Christian I looked up to. Never swearing or yelling, he was able to gain respect through his actions. Around Coach Stirtz, I not only played hard, but I carried myself with dignity and respect as well." It's funny, I don't remember Coach Stirtz being someone who was a "Bible Beater", however I do remember Christianity being a pillar of his life. How he carried himself as a coach, looking back now, really showed that his walk with Christ was strong. I believe we all have someone that when looking back on our life to this point, we remember as a Coach Stirtz. It may or may not be an actual coach in sports but maybe a coach in life that had the same impact on you.

Pause now and take the time to think back. Then, identify a Christian that you know in your life that may not be a *Bible Beater* but one who you know is walking the walk, talking the talk.

_____

_____

Next, expound a little bit on the characteristics you remember or maybe still see that make them standout as a Christian?

_____

_____

_____

Way to go. Are you beginning to see the potential power of your choice in the role models for your life?

2. A turning point in my life, in the use of drugs, was when I dislocated my elbow. I was first given a shot of morphine in the ambulance. Then the doctor prescribed a bottle of Percocet. Both were given to relieve the excruciating pain in my elbow. I was unaware, at that time, that taking the Percocet would also help relieve another pain in my life. Not a physical pain but a mental pain, an emotional pain. That was the underlying pain brought on from the fighting between my mother and stepfather. That pain was leading to unknown resentment. In hindsight, I have been able to see that having the Percocet relieve that underlying pain, even if only temporarily, along with the pain in my elbow, became my first mental link of opioids in addiction. Then came the desire to have the temporary relief become permanent. What a revelation it was for me to see this.

Today, because of the human havoc that the opioid epidemic has had, many doctors are now better trained through questioning to deal with a patient's underlying *pain* that creates a *void* waiting to be filled.

Some simple questions would have probably revealed this *void* that was growing within me. The *void* created by my inability to have any impact on my mother and stepfather's fighting. Yet, those questions never came and were never dealt with other than my own choice to relieve or fill the *void* with drugs.

In reading this I will bet that some of your own pain and *voids* have come to the forefront of your thought. Those things, maybe similar to mine, that happened in your life that seemed to create a need for relief or a *void* desired to be filled, made whole, made right.

Pause and identify a person(s) or event(s) that you feel created your *void* or became a contributing factor(s) to your "Perfect Storm" of addiction.

_____
_____
_____
_____
_____

Now, can you see this as an underlying pain that the drugs or alcohol help relieve, only to return when you sobered up?

____ Yes    ____ No

Do you feel you are now better able to recognize those things and the impact they had upon you? Write about it.

_____
_____
_____
_____
_____

Congratulations, though this may seem a short day, it is one of the most impactful days in your deliverance from the Perfect Storm of addiction!

I continue to be proud of you. Breath for a bit, digest, then read Chapter 6 and get ready for Day 8. See you there.

# DAY 8

## CHAPTER 6

Welcome back to Day 8. With the fresh revelation of how voids and pains are filled and relieved by your actions, dig in here to feel that connection with Cody. Continue your journey head on.

Allow the Good Lord to continue His work in you today by opening up with the Petition Prayer with Thanksgiving:

*"Dear Lord, I enter this prayer in the name of Your son Jesus Christ. I pray and thank You for allowing my faith in You to come alive in me as I continue through this 30-day program. I know that it is by faith that I continue forward, as I'm seeking something that sometimes feels impossible to conquer. By trusting You, I know that anything is possible including faith in being delivered from drugs and alcohol. Your word says, "For by Grace you have been saved through faith." Father, I believe that by my faith in You, You will deliver me. In Jesus Christ's name, Amen."*

Having re-read Chapter 6, you are ready to begin.

## THE EXECUTIONER'S PORTAL ...INWARD

1. "My brethren, count it all joy when you fall into various trials, knowing that the testing of your faith produces patience. But let patience have it's perfect work, that you may be perfect and complete, lacking nothing." James 1:2-4

On page 84, I once again mention the Faith and Courage tattoos on my triceps. In this part of my story, it had been several years since I'd had them inked. There is substance to faith. That substance is the very thing you hope for, in this case you, <u>being</u> *Delivered* from addiction.

Faith is also the "evidence of things not seen", in this case you, <u>living</u> *Delivered* from addiction. We began this discussion of faith in Day 1 when I referenced the quote from Hebrews 11:1 that Ellen shared in her Foreword.

Maybe you can't physically see God working in your life in either capacity at this very moment. Yet, it is the faith in that, yet to be seen, which is carrying you on through this program, believing that soon you will be delivered.

God will do what He promises. What are His promises? God's promises are in His Word or what He speaks to you that is consistent with His Word. If you ask God to deliver you from your addiction, hold strong, keep the faith, He is on it. Just because you can't see the effects immediately, trust that God is answering your prayers. Want proof? You, having this program in your hand, and your commitment to work the program, are two powerful pieces of evidence that God is answering you.

A large part of faith is patience, as the scripture above from James 1:2-4 says. Only when we fully trust God, do we surrender to Him. When this happens, we are perfected in His Son, Jesus Christ. In other words, if you are seeking deliverance from the tugging of sobriety, and it hasn't yet happened, continue to be faithful. Your faithfulness will produce the patience needed to be delivered. I am confident, without a doubt, God will deliver you.

Please repeat this prayer of patience:

*"Lord God, I come to you today faithful. I pray for patience as I continue to work on being fully delivered from addiction. Father, I know that without faith, I will not be able to obtain the patience needed to receive deliverance from my addictions. Only you can provide this patience. I put my faith in you Father, waiting patiently on all that I ask in faith. In Jesus Christ's name, Amen."*

## ...OUTWARD

2. On page 89 I speak of myself when I say, "Unblinking, he continued in a fixated glare, unaware of the horror movie posters in front of him. They had gone from being horrible to being normal." As I wrote this for the book, I was recognizing a phenomenon had been taking place. That when I allowed Satan and his voice to become close, and I distanced myself from God and His Voice, it was interesting how differently I began to see things that I once thought macabre. Whether it was the 'horror movie posters' that I mention above, or the demonic tattoos slowly becoming etched onto my skin, I recognized that I had begun to accept the darkness and allow it a place inside my head. My sense is that you have your own moments that are coming into view as you read of mine.

Pause here, be open and honest with yourself and write about them as I once did.

What are some things you can identify that you wish you wouldn't have allowed a place in your head and into your life?

_____
_____
_____
_____
_____
_____
_____
_____
_____

Way to go. Once again you have done the challenging work. Bringing it into the light of truth is carrying you forward. Take some time to digest this, then get ready for Day 9 by reading Downward and Too Far Again.

See you soon.

# DAY 9

## CHAPTER 6

Here we go, Day 9. As you come off of the challenging answers to your Day 8, let us be thankful. We are on this journey together. Let us begin with our daily prayer:

*"Dear Lord, I enter this prayer in the name of Your son Jesus Christ. I pray and thank You for allowing my faith in You to come alive in me as I continue through this 30-day program. I know that it is by faith that I continue forward, as I'm seeking something that sometimes feels impossible to conquer. By trusting You, I know that anything is possible including faith in being delivered from drugs and alcohol. Your word says, "For by Grace you have been saved through faith." Father, I believe that by my faith in You, You will deliver me. In Jesus Christ's name, Amen."*

Now you are fully armed, let's continue what came after Cody went Outward.

### THE EXECUTIONER'S PORTAL ...DOWNWARD

1. "For I know the thoughts that I think toward you, says the Lord, thoughts of peace and not of evil, to give you a future and a

hope." Jeremiah 29:11

On page 96 I continue to speak of myself saying, "Cody, now thinking he was asleep, saw himself in a dream of being incarcerated. A dream of going to prison." Wow, If what Jeremiah says above is true and the Lord's thoughts are "…not of evil…," like the ones I was having of going to prison, then where did they come from? If the Lord's thoughts are "…of Peace…and of hope." then where did the dream of being incarcerated come from? In answering these many questions, I came to see that when we begin to have these thoughts, it is very important that we work to recognize where they are coming from, and what is producing them. If we do not do so then over time, these thoughts get played in our mind until we've accepted them fully true, as if a premonition of our life and future. If it comes with a ray of hope and encouragement to turn one's life around, then that is from God. If it is filled with fear and shame and guilt, then it is from the enemy.

Maybe you can relate. Maybe, like me, they were thoughts of going to prison. Or, maybe you're thinking of other negative consequences that you've allowed to play out so many times in your mind, that you have accepted them as true and premonitions of your life and future.

Pause right here and take some time to delve into this.

Identify a thought with a consequence, or two, that seems to be constantly playing in your mind, as if allowing you to accept its very possibility.

_____

_____

_____

Write out where you believe those thoughts are coming from?

_____
_____
_____

Now, say a prayer asking the Good Lord to give you some new thoughts and language for your future. Listen carefully and when you hear them, write them down. (They may not come immediately but they will come. If so, return her to record them.)

_____
_____
_____

## ...TOO FAR I GO!

On page 99, I begin to share with you my mind:

"I wasn't thinking about dying. I never had done that. All I ever seemed to consciously care about was the present moments that existed. Sitting there on the couch I had become paralyzed, frozen in time as she grabbed me, comforted me. I laid back. Her security, a spider's web. Soon to be trapped, she began whispering words that rationalized the havoc she was soon to inflict. "Close your eyes", she whispered. I complied. Her touch, warm and soothing. All the problems that existed in my life were for an instant gone...forgotten."

I continue sharing into page 100:

"I knew this kind of high had an enormous cost but as she surged through my veins it was all justified. My body, now a puppet of flesh and bone controlled by its master, Fentanyl. I needed her more than anything and now I had her. I may question friends, family, even myself, but at least I knew I had her. There was nothing more important than this high. She understood me, sympathized. She made rock bottom a place of peace, less cold and lonely. Her seeds were now planted as I could feel my eyes beginning to roll back into my head. Wondering if it was her destructive path that was slowly and methodically edging its way through my sure-to-be a lifeless body if she succeeded. Was another victim about to be thrown to the wolves? Would my pound of flesh be ravenously eaten? Would I be pulled apart with greedy chomps? I felt like I was waiting to be devoured, clueless like the lamb sent to slaughter. My chest, no longer rising and falling with my breath. She's upon me now. Her weight, one of immovable force. I fight against her as I realize her intentions. But she's too strong for my weakened state. She wraps her long fingers around my throat and squeezes, cutting off my air like a plunge into an icy lake, Fentanyl. The Executioner. As I overdose, everything goes black. I succumb."

This was actually written long before anything else in the book ever was. When the time came to express in words what "Too Far I Go!" looked like for in the book, I pulled this from a section of my diary that I had written a year before. At the time of its initial writing, I was still very much controlled by my addiction, and it's evident in the darkness of it. It was my best attempt at trying to get somebody who doesn't know anything about drugs, to understand an overdose. I also felt this was very important for other addicts to hear if I was ever going to be able to help them in their deliverance from some of the same.

## DAY 9

At this point in your 30-day program, it's your opportunity to journal about your addiction. Be creative. Possibly begin by explaining what it's like for you to be controlled by a substance. Go ahead and give your best. Take your time but get it out. You, like I, will be glad you did.

_____
_____
_____
_____
_____
_____
_____
_____
_____
_____
_____
_____
_____
_____

Now breathe. You have done a fine job. Rest knowing it will be used to empower you moving forward.

When you are ready, delve into Chapter 7 and I will see you soon.

# DAY 10

## CHAPTER 7

Welcome back from your journaling. You are now on Day 10. You have reached a milestone, even if you do not recognize it. See most people never get this far in any Program that requires personal introspection and change. Yet, you have done just that. Your commitment is amazing! Be happy for yourself and continue to believe in yourself, as God believes in you!

Let's get started by saying your daily prayer:

*"Dear Lord, I enter this prayer in the name of Your son Jesus Christ. I pray and thank You for allowing my faith in You to come alive in me as I continue through this 30-day program. I know that it is by faith that I continue forward, as I'm seeking something that sometimes feels impossible to conquer. By trusting You, I know that anything is possible including faith in being delivered from drugs and alcohol. Your word says, "For by Grace you have been saved through faith." Father, I believe that by my faith in You, You will deliver me. In Jesus Christ's name, Amen."*

Here you go…

## THE EXECUTIONER'S VOICE ...TOO MUCH

1. "Therefore God also gave them up to uncleanness, in the lusts of their hearts, to dishonor their bodies among themselves, who exchanged the truth of God for the lie, and worshipped and served the creature rather than the Creator, who is blessed forever. Amen" Romans 1:24-25

"If God had bigger plans for Cody, he hadn't yet uncovered them," page 103 says.

I was using and selling drugs, getting tattoos, having sex with different women, doing every vile thing, and at the same time, wondering why God wasn't working in my life. Looking back now, it's easy to see why. I had, like the scripture from Romans says, "exchanged the truth of God for the lie." I was indeed worshipping and serving "the creature rather than the Creator." Maybe you can relate.

Are you wanting God to move mightily in your life, yet you're still partaking in sin?

Are you waiting for a break in your life, yet still using drugs and alcohol?

Watch how mightily God will move in your life when you begin to live in "the truth" rather than "the lie." I can honestly say, even within my incarceration, God is moving mountains in my life. I'm at peace and filled with more joy than I ever have been. "But how is that possible Cody, you're in prison?" you may be asking. The truth is, God will also move mightily in your life if you simply 'turn' from your addiction, surrender it to God, and begin living a Christ filled life. Will you say this prayer with me?

*"Lord God, help me turn from the lie I've been living as I surrender my addiction to you. Father, help me to walk in the truth rather than the lie. I'm ready to start living a Christ filled life of peace, hope, joy and love Father. I ask for Your Power and Strength to begin this process in me, right now in the name of your precious Son, Jesus Christ. Amen."*

What you prayed and how you prayed was in fact taking the power of addiction to the cross. I encourage you stop right now, take your Bible, and revisit Colossians 2:13-15 to receive the visual of who you are, what you just did, and the understanding of what God has done with the addictive principalities and powers of Satan that once controlled you.

Once you have read it and found its relationship to you and what just happened, take a moment, and rewrite the experience in your own words.

_____

_____

_____

_____

_____

This is what it means to have God working in your life.

2. "Every Valley shall be exalted
   And every mountain and hill brought low;
   The crooked places shall be made straight
   And the rough places smooth;"
   Isaiah 40:4

I once again speak of myself on page 103 saying, "Taking the path of least resistance, or no resistance at all, he had reverted easily back to his old ways, full steam ahead!"

The path to sobriety seems impossible, especially in the midst of our addictions. Continuing to use drugs and alcohol seems like a much easier path than trying to quit. This however is a lie. (And you are beginning to know where those lies are coming from, right?)

You see, after we place our faith in Jesus Christ, He begins working the impossible. He makes every path the path of least resistance. Like the scripture from Isaiah says, "The crooked places shall be made straight." What seems impossible, begins to seem anything but impossible 'In Christ's. As Christ says in Matthew 11:30, "For My yoke is easy, and My burden is light." "*In Christ*" all the barriers and hurdles in your life are taken down.

I want you to take some time and write a list of things in your life you think to be "impossible." Then go back through that list and next to every single one you think to be impossible, write "is possible with God" next to it.

Example: To quit using drugs (is possible with God)

1. _____
_____
_____
_____

2. _____
_____
_____
_____

3. _____
   _____
   _____
   _____

Use your separate journal if you have more to add.

## ...TOO DEEP

3. "And even as they did not like to retain God in their knowledge, God gave them over to a debased mind, to do those things which are not fitting;" Romans 1:28

On page 110 I mention that I had, "been building resentment towards women." It wasn't just women I was resenting either. There was a whole host of people in my life that I carried the burden of resentment towards. The further I distance myself from God, the more of a "debased" mind I obtained. This was my mind filled with many of the things listed by the Apostle Paul in Romans. Further down in that scripture, Paul mentions "unforgiveness" as one of them.

However, when I allowed Jesus Christ into my life, not only did resentment turn to forgiveness, but addiction turned to deliverance. This, in-turn resulted in my life of sobriety. How amazing this was, is, and will be for my life!

This very thing can, is, and will happen for you as you allow Jesus Christ into your life. This gift was not reserved for me alone my friend, it is reserved for you as well. Seek to allow more of Him in into your life every day.

Pause and make a list of people you feel you're holding resentment towards, including why are you holding such resentment?

1. _____
_____

2. _____
_____

3. _____
_____

4. _____
_____

Once again, use your separate journal if you have more to add.

4. On page 115, I notice a picture of Jesus in the tattoo shop and speak of what I see as, "The picture of Jesus wearing His crown of thorns. The same picture he had seen on the calendar in his Boys Town office. Cody and Jesus again stared at each other for what seemed to him like an eternity, as if oblivious to the other tattoo guns buzzing and the music blaring. The other people coming and going into the shop, all unnoticed in this surreal moment as Cody gulped down the spit in his throat. He could have heard a needle drop through the noise. Time froze as he stared at the picture of Jesus."

I grew up Catholic, but only later in life did I realize what Jesus actually did for me that day He went to the cross. You see, before Jesus, I couldn't really have a relationship with God because of my sinful nature. God loved me so much, He sent his only begotten Son to die and bare those sins for me. Jesus took the weight of all sin and died with it so that I could also have a relationship with God. Jesus Christ was the last sacrifice so that I could have an opportunity to be saved from the penalty of sin, that being eternal death.

Of course, there I was in a tattoo shop oblivious to all of this. Because the truth is this: If I had any idea what Jesus Christ did for me on the cross, I surely wouldn't be in a tattoo shop or using drugs for that matter.

This same type of situation has or is happening to you. Yet, the good news is that the same realization is available for you as well. The realization of what Jesus has done for you.

Pause here and really think about this next question. When you are ready write out your response.

Make a list of what you believe Jesus has personally done for you in your life.

1. _____
_____
2. _____
_____
3. _____
_____
4. _____
_____

Go to your journal if you need more space. It is important to write out all that you believe Jesus has done for you.

5. On page 117 I say about myself as I sit in my car, "For a minute he felt like quitting as the voice put in his head, "I should call someone and tell them everything. Lauren? Mom? or Dad? Anyone!" He scrolled to his mom's number on his phone. His thumb millimeters above the screen, he could almost feel the smooth plastic. Yet, an impenetrable force field between his thumb and screen remained."

Today is an important day in your 30-day program. Today you're going to be stronger than I was on the day I wrote about that. Today you're going say a short prayer for God's Guidance and then go get out your phone and reach out to someone you love. You are going to tell them, leave them a message, or send them a text message saying, "I have enrolled in a 30 Days to Life Deliverance Program. It is my 10th day, and I am in the process of being delivered from my bondage to addiction! I love you." After that, you will respond however you feel "Guided" to do so. Remember the Good Lord is on board with you.

Ready....set.... Go!!!

Now, take a moment and write out who you called, how it went, and how you now feel in doing so.

_____
_____
_____
_____
_____

I am incredibly proud of you for taking this step. Your strength 'In Christ's is clearly growing daily.

Now, let's move on to be sure you remember what happened to me when I didn't do what you just did.

## ...TOO FAR, AGAIN!

6. "For the wages of sin is death,
   But the gift of God is eternal
   life in Christ Jesus our Lord."
   Romans 6:23

On page 120 I go on to say, "I was graduating from user to addict. From an addict to Junkie. From junkie to possessed. All of the reality of it came rushing together at that very moment in my kitchen."
I am explaining that my addiction was now something much worse than before.

Throughout the book, I really try to help you understand how smoothly and methodically Satan moves in. How he works to take up permanent residence inside your head. How he deceitfully works a voice of a lie into a truth so as to have you act in areas it would be better not to. You find me referring to that voice as "she," but she is actually Satan in disguise in my mind.

Satan speaks in many different ways if you allow him to. Yes, you play a part in allowing him in. And just when you don't think it can get worse as an addict, it does, proving his manipulative ways once again. It is a constant battle that you know all too well. It is a battle that he knows you cannot win alone. He works overtime once he has you in his grip to not recognize this truth. He convinces you over and over again that you can handle it, you can deal with it, you don't need anyone else!

Yet, the loving power of God is greater. Soon, you will find yourself in a place to receive the truth, that you have the Greatest Strength available to you when you surrender it to God, through Jesus Christ.

Then comes the revelation that by placing your faith in Jesus Christ, you are saved from death. And not just a physical death but saved from an eternal separation from God. When I finally cleared my head and thought about this, I couldn't imagine a worse position to be in, an eternal separation like that. It was then that I surrendered and embraced the Power of the Holy Spirit, His Power in me.

When you place your faith in Jesus Christ, He begins working in your life immediately. He is the ultimate healer and immediately begins cleaning house and Satan has to go!! Those that come to Jesus are in good company, He has a 100% success rate. Will you stop right now and say this prayer with me?

*"In the name of Jesus Christ, I give you all authority over my life. Satan you have no power over my life from this point forward. All principalities and powers of darkness were rendered useless the day You died on the cross for my sins. They were brought to light by The One that is Light Father. I am saved from an eternal separation from God, and I have been given the gift of eternal life. In the name of Jesus Christ, Satan I renounce you, your lies, and the tricks that you attempt to play on my mind. In the name of Jesus Christ, Amen."*

Now, call it a day knowing you are leaving the program Empowered by the Holy Spirit in you. Praise God!

Be sure to read Chapter 8 and I will see you when you enter Day 11.

# DAY 11

## CHAPTER 8

Hello again my friend. Welcome to Day 11. I Trust you have read Chapter 8 and are ready to continue your Deliverance Journey.

Let's build on the habit you have now created by saying your daily prayer:

"Dear Lord, I enter this prayer in the name of Your son Jesus Christ. I pray and thank You for allowing my faith in You to come alive in me as I continue through this 30-day program. I know that it is by faith that I continue forward, as I'm seeking something that sometimes feels impossible to conquer. By trusting You, I know that anything is possible including faith in being delivered from drugs and alcohol. Your word says, "For by Grace you have been saved through faith." Father, I believe that by my faith in You, You will deliver me. In Jesus Christ's name, Amen."

Here you go…

**THE SEARCH FOR EQUILIBRIUM
…WITH-IN THE FAMILY**

1. "When I was a child, I spoke as a child, I understood as a child, I thought as a child, but when I became a man, I put away childish

things." 1Corinthians 13:11

In this entire section of the book, I write from the perspective of when I was a very young boy. When I wrote this section, it was very interesting to discover what came out on paper. I had never written from this perspective before, and what I wrote surprised even me. Why did I even choose to write from this young perspective? I later learned that the child I rediscovered in my writings, had been living in me all the way up until I was delivered from my addiction. If you're struggling with an addiction, chances are that you too hold a child within you, waiting to be rediscovered. That child inside can be the very thing that is limiting your growth. Like the scripture above from 1Corinthians seems to imply, if we continue to speak, understand, and think as a child does, we remain like a child in those areas. In this exercise, I want you to write about a time in your life when you were very young. It can be about anything. Then, answer the questions that follow. Begin, "When I was a child…"

_____
_____
_____
_____
_____
_____
_____
_____
_____

Very good. Now here are the questions:

1. What did you discover as you wrote about your younger self?

_____
_____
_____
_____
_____

2. Was there anyone you harbored resentment towards? If so, why?

_____
_____
_____
_____

3. Was the memory a good memory or a not so good memory? Why?

_____
_____
_____
_____

4. Do you feel as if a part of this child still lives within you? Why? How so?

_____
_____
_____
_____

Good Job. Way to go deep and open up to those personal things.

## ...WITH-IN THE COACHES

2. "Behold what manner of love the Father has bestowed on us, that we should be called children of God!" 1 John 3:1

In this section of the book, I discuss my insatiable drive to not only impress my coaches but impress my mother as well. I loved her more than anything, and to this day, she's still a significant figure in my life. I hope you can imagine what kind of support she has been for me as a mother and a friend during my incarceration. Yet, as a child with a tumultuous upbringing, our relationship wasn't always as strong as it is now, especially after being delivered from the addiction of drugs. However, in those days, I often did some pretty outlandish things to get her attention. Between my stepfather, three sisters, brother, and a demanding job, I often did whatever I could to get her attention. I craved her love. But what if I told you that the Most High parent was already showing me all the love I needed? Only later, after going to prison and while being delivered from the addiction of drugs, did I learn that my Father in heaven called me to be a child of His, Yes, a child of God. That's one of the most amazing facts about placing your faith in Jesus Christ, His Father also calls you to be a child of His. Worldly love and affection from our parents are great, but would you believe me if I told you they aren't necessary? You may think I'm crazy, but I can put to rest the Nature vs. Nurture debate right here and right now: Placing your faith in Jesus Christ, who made the nature, will most certainly nurture you as well. You're in safe keeping as a child of God.

Luke 12:7 says, "But, the very hairs of your head are all numbered. Do not fear therefore; you are more valued than many sparrows."

## DAY 11

You'd better believe that the hairs on your head are numbered.

No adversity will come to you without His say so. When we allow the enemy access to our lives, we enter a different jurisdiction and God cannot, because of his perfect justice nature, trespass on the enemy's property. Adversity will come and when it does, God uses it to grow and bless us when we are in contract with God in the same way. Furthermore, through prayer and fellowship with the Father, you don't need worldly praise and worldly attention to know your value. All the attention and gratification you need as proof that you are loved, was laid right there on the cross.

In this exercise, I want you to write a letter to God. Thank Him for loving you and believing that you're loved enough to send His Son to die on the cross. Finish it up with what that love means to you.

_____
_____
_____
_____
_____
_____
_____
_____

Now, take some time to rest in His love. Then finish reading Chapter 8 and I will see you at Day 12.

# DAY 12

## CHAPTER 8

Welcome to Day 12. You are ready to wrap up Chapter 8.

Remember to get with God and pray:

"Dear Lord, I enter this prayer in the name of Your son Jesus Christ. I pray and thank You for allowing my faith in You to come alive in me as I continue through this 30-day program. I know that it is by faith that I continue forward, as I'm seeking something that sometimes feels impossible to conquer. By trusting You, I know that anything is possible including faith in being delivered from drugs and alcohol. Your word says, "For by Grace you have been saved through faith." Father, I believe that by my faith in You, You will deliver me. In Jesus Christ's name, Amen."

Alright, lets continue…

## THE SEARCH FOR EQUILIBRIUM ...WITH-IN MYSELF

1. "If my parents had found an alternative to forgiveness, so could I. "Why forgive when you can forget? Why forgive when there are so many more alternatives?" I surmised. Divorce seemed to be a decent enough alternative to forgiveness, lots of parents did it?"

This you find me writing on page 141. The truth, I later learned, is that there is no effective alternative to forgiveness. Choosing to 'not forgive' someone doesn't make the problem go away, instead the anger and hurt remains, either exposed or hidden. Furthermore, to not forgive primarily hurts you, not the person you are harboring resentment towards in hopes of hurting. In most cases the person that you 'feel' has wronged you, or who actually did wrong you, couldn't care less if you forgive them or not. They keep going about their business as if unfazed by the event. Then, when we do make the decision to forgive them, most of us do it only on an intellectual level. "Intellectual Forgiveness" isn't real because humans seem to lack the ability to truly forgive the person and pain of the infraction. They intellectually say they forgive the person, but the sting of the infraction is set aside in a mental compartment. It sits there ready to be pulled back out to be added to any future infraction by that same person. Long story short, we must give the person, and their infraction over to God in prayer, to experience true lifelong forgiveness. You are going to learn what that looks like and how to do that later on in your 30-day program. But for now, think of a person or persons you feel you're currently harboring resentment and unforgiveness towards. Then pause and take a few moments and write out why you haven't been able to fully forgive that person as of today? (Be as specific and detailed because you will be returning to this when called upon later in the program.)

_____

_____

_____

_____

Good job. Be encouraged to know resolution in forgiveness will come soon.

## ...WITH-IN THE WEIGHTS

2. In this section of the book, I talk about sports and lifting weights as being my initial drug to fill a growing void within me. Most of us can probably pinpoint talents or activities we engaged in that filled our voids, long before drugs did. It's not a surprise to me when I hear about the previous successes that those struggling with drugs or alcohol had long before they tried drugs or alcohol. Just like me, many were leaders in their high schools in either academics or sports. Many were extremely good writers, poets, or painters. Many were successful in their work, quickly becoming successful in their respected fields. Then, when a void seems unfilled and drugs and/or alcohol are introduced into their lives, everything comes crashing down. The drugs and/or alcohol slowly take the place of the talent or activity they once held so dear to them. My hunch is that you are relating to this as you read it.

Please pause right now and write about your most memorable experience, achievement and or success that was part of your life before you found your addiction taking over to fill a void.

_____
_____
_____
_____
_____
_____

Congratulations, you have dug deep once again. Be assured you will be revisiting these areas and find resolution to them as you grow in your deliverance.

Let this settle for a bit then, when you are ready, re-read Chapter 9 and begin your Day 13.

# DAY 13

## CHAPTER 9

Welcome to Day 13! If you have re-read Chapter 9 then you are ready for your 'get started' daily prayer:

"Dear Lord, I enter this prayer in the name of Your son Jesus Christ. I pray and thank You for allowing my faith in You to come alive in me as I continue through this 30-day program. I know that it is by faith that I continue forward, as I'm seeking something that sometimes feels impossible to conquer. By trusting You, I know that anything is possible including faith in being delivered from drugs and alcohol. Your word says, "For by Grace you have been saved through faith." Father, I believe that by my faith in You, You will deliver me. In Jesus Christ's name, Amen."

Ok, now that you have been reminded that you have the Greatest on board (The Holy Spirit), let's go.

## THE DEEPER DARKER STATE OF MIND…
## …LESSNESS

1. "If we confess our sins, He is faithful and just to forgive us our sins and to cleanse us from all unrighteousness."
1John 1:9

On page 145 you find me talking about myself saying, "Driving in his car Cody found himself asking God for forgiveness. His sin, now much more significant than when he was the boy asking the Priest to forgive him for pushing his little sister off her bike. He was in much deeper than in those days. His place of confession, no longer a booth in the back of the Church. It was now a car, his car. He asked God directly "Forgive me for the overdose, the drug dealing, the womanizing, and everything else that has come of my life?"

Placing your faith in Jesus Christ means that you "are" forgiven. It's one of the greatest pillars of Christianity. When God sent His Son Jesus Christ to die on the cross, He bore the sins for all humanity: past, present, and future. However, this doesn't mean you've been given "free rein" to continue in sin simply because you've forgiven. The Apostle Paul says it best in Romans 6:1: "What shall we say then? Shall we continue in sin that grace may abound? Certainly not!" This does mean however that when you do find yourself in sin, you should confess your sin to God, through Jesus Christ. It is God's Holy Spirit in your heart that pricks you, tugs at you, or prods you to know that you have indeed sinned, broken fellowship, or transgressed which leads to the desire to confess it.

Here is a great analogy for you: Confessing your sin allows you to maintain right fellowship with God. It's like a father and his son. If the son does something bad in school and the principal calls the house, the father is aware that his son has misbehaved. However, when his son comes home from school, the father is hoping that his son will confess what he did in school without him having to ask. The father is hoping for honesty, maturity, and responsibility in his sons' actions. If his son does confess his misbehavior, the son will be dealt with accordingly and he will be forgiven. On the other hand, if the son does not confess what he did, he will be dealt with a bit differently, yet still be forgiven. See the difference is in the son, not the father. Confession frees the son, not the father. In either case he still remains the son of his loving father. A similar relationship works with us and God. God allows us to confess our sins, through Jesus Christ, to remain in constant fellowship with Him. Through all my sin, I was convicted to confess my sin on that day in my car. That, my friends, was the silver lining in this chapter. The Holy Spirit that dwells inside us, also convicts us on a daily basis that if we sin, need to confess our sin and remain in fellowship with God. The Holy Spirit is our moral compass. Once again, He is that something inside you convicting you to confess your sin to God.

If you feel pricked, tugged, or provoked in the spirit to do so, at this point in your 30-day program, I'd like you to confess your sin to Jesus Christ now. I suggest writing it down for you to be able to visually see the very thing you will be released from. If you would rather hold it inside that is for you to choose.

_____

_____

_____

_____

Now finish your confession with: *"Dear Heavenly Father Thank You for being faithful and just to have forgiven me of my sin and cleansed me from all unrighteousness surrounding it. In Jesus' Name. Amen."*

2. "So Jesus said to them, "Because of your unbelief; for assuredly, I say to you, if you have faith as a mustard seed, you will say to this mountain, 'Move from here to there,' and it will move; and nothing will be impossible for you." Matthew 17:20

"Are you listening?" he asked God. "What if my faith isn't strong enough?" you hear me say on page 147. My understanding is that there is no meter on faith. It was later in prison that I learned this valuable piece for my delivered walk "In Christ." Jesus Himself said that all we need is faith the size of a of mustard seed to experience the impossible for our lives. If you've ever seen a mustard seed, you know they are extremely small, and I believe this is why Jesus used this exact seed as an example of faith. That day in my car, I can now tell you that I probably didn't even have that much faith. As you can tell in reading my voice, I was wavering. God doesn't want us to waiver. When we question our own faith in God, what are we questioning about God Himself? Do you believe He can do the impossible for you in your life?

\_\_\_\_ Yes \_\_\_\_No

In whatever way you responded just now, stop, and answer these questions:

1. What do you need to do right now to strengthen your faith?

_____

_____

_____

2. What do you need to do in the future to ensure you remain faithful?

_____

_____

_____

3. What is a major roadblock in your faithfulness in Jesus Christ?

_____

_____

_____

3. Then Jesus said to those Jews who believed Him, "If you abide in my word, you are My disciples indeed. And you shall know the truth, and the truth shall make you free." John 8:31-32

Once again you find me speaking of myself on page 149 saying, "He knew he was no different from millions of Christians all over America. Hailing God till they reach Hell. Cody wouldn't be surprised how he got there though. He smiled, thinking about the present-day 'Christian.' They all pray as good Christians do. An outward fraud that eventually holds no water with God. "He knows what you're doing, and He knows the truth," Cody thought."

What is "The Truth" in reference to the scripture above from John? Let me help you here, "The Truth" is God's Word. And what is God's Word? God's Word is everything that is written in The Holy Bible. Jesus instructs us to abide, or "live" in His Word. On page 149 I mention being frustrated at the present-day Christian's ability to abide in The Word and to live by "The Truth." As a drug addict and dealer, I believed I was accepting my fate in Hell. By His Word,

I have come to learn that as a believer of Jesus Christ, even at that time in my transgression as an addict or dealer, Hell was not where I would be going. In looking back what I found to be true was that I was in fact a Christian that wasn't "abiding" in His word, His Truth. I am sure you are seeing that now while reading and studying me. It is my hope that you are coming to the same revelation of yourself and are beginning to see what deliverance is. How ironic is it that The Truth is what sets us free, yet I was living a life as far away from The Truth as I could possibly get? Instead, I was living a gigantic lie. It's no wonder I write these very words from a prison cell, ignoring for so long the thing that could have set me free, The Truth.

Pause right now and express your answer to these questions:

What are some things that you believe are keeping you from experiencing The Truth?

_____
_____
_____

What do you believe is allowing you to remain in bondage? (It doesn't have to be just an addiction to drugs and alcohol, it can be anything you feel that is holding you back in your life.)

_____
_____
_____

4. "But what does it say? "The word is near you, in your mouth and in your heart"(that is, the word of faith which we preach): that if you confess with your mouth the Lord Jesus and believe in your

heart that God has raised Him from the dead, you will be saved." Romans 10:8,9

"They love to do the easy shit and pray. How many of you so-called Christians are walking the walk too? Putting in the work to help humanity? Cody wondered." You read of my cynical tone on page 150. You will also again notice that I do not appear to see myself in the camp of the Christians. Nor had I rededicated my life to God through Jesus Christ. That would come in time. By this time in my revelation of my life in the book and in this program, I pray you've received Jesus Christ into your life. If you have not, there is no better time than now to do so. Follow the direction of Romans 10:8-9 and confess with your mouth, "Jesus is Lord and I believe in my heart that God raised Him from the dead," and be saved to a delivered life. If you have already done this prior to your addiction, within your addiction, or post addiction, then take a moment to rededicate and recommit yourself to the truth of Romans 10:9.

In this choice you have found that the fundamental pillar of Christianity is placing your faith in Jesus Christ as your Lord and Savior, receiving God's free gift of salvation. When this occurred, you also received The Holy Spirit into your heart and God became available for working new wonders in your life. Welcome to the Kingdom my friend.

"But someone will say, "You have faith, and I have works." Show me your faith without your works, and I will show you my faith by my works." James 2:18

In regard to addiction, or any bondage for that matter, God begins loosening those shackles immediately. If you've received The Holy

Spirit by placing your faith in Jesus Christ, and you open your eyes, ears, hands and mouth to His presence, you'll begin to notice not only the changes in your personal life in regard to addiction, but also the changes you begin to make in other's lives as well. This is what we see James meaning by "works" for our lives. Let us begin to see "works" as the outward illumination of God, through the Holy Spirit, by how we live, act, interact, and perform works of charity with others, to name of few.

Paul actually names these as the "Fruit of the Spirit" in Galatians 5:22,23 saying, "But the fruit of the Spirit is love, joy, peace, long-suffering, kindness, goodness, faithfulness, gentleness, self-control. Against such there is no law." This fruit of the Spirit has been planted in your heart and is available for you to draw upon at your will. Therefore, knowing this, if your faith is strong, so will be your works, or acts of good deeds as they will emanate from the "Fruit."

That day in my car, I expressed my frustration at the present-day Christian's "works." Clearly it was a pre-judgmental mindset from my addictive self as I drove by. It was easier to do that than accept that I was a Christian living out that very accusation. My hope is that others may not have the same off hand opinion of me today in my post addiction delivered state. I have come to learn that being a solider of Jesus Christ's army doesn't mean we should go to Church on Sundays and call it a week. Being a Holy Spirit Christian means, we are called to have the light of Jesus Christ shining in us, in how we live and how we interact with others. Yes, it takes removing the pattern of your old self, having a new spirit of your mind, and practicing, practicing, practicing the new self that you are "In Christ." Take a few moments and refer to the Bible passage of Ephesians

4:22,23,24 to recognize that Paul is speaking of you and me today! Amazing, isn't it?

This week, as you continue forward in your 30-day program, I challenge you to do just that, going above and beyond your Sunday Worship. Here are some examples of some things you can do right in your local community. Pray for Guidance, then begin anew. Maybe you have some of your own ideas as well. Add them to this list and make a commitment to begin to practice those behaviors and activities. You do not have to do them all, but you do have to get started.

1. Volunteer at a homeless shelter or soup kitchen.
2. Hold the door for someone.
3. Donate a few dollars to a local charity.
4. Tell someone about Jesus Christ.
5. Buy a Bible for a friend.
6. Call someone you haven't called for a while; tell them you miss them.
7. Fellowship with someone you are pricked to do so.
8. _____
9. _____
10. _____

5. "To Him who rides on the heaven
of heavens, which were of old!
Indeed, He sends out His voice,
a mighty voice."
Psalm 68:33

On page 152 I continue to share my mind saying, "Cody thought and decided two things. One, God was indeed talking back through his speakers, sending him signs he should bail, 'quit' everything. This wasn't football or another sport. It was something he could quit. He could quit. "In this case, it's ok to quit Cody, he told himself as if to permit himself the thought." On this day, I was certain God was attempting to speak to me through a Tupac song. It seemed that God was doing everything He could to prevent me from going to prison, or worse, dying. As was writing those very words from a prison cell, I realize I had been ignoring all of His nudges. I had allowed a smaller voice, her voice to override His. This may be tough stuff to look at for sure, but it is very important to do so, nonetheless.

I'm going to challenge you to think hard at this moment. I have a great belief that God has been telling you something persistently, like He was me. He is speaking as if to say "Stop! Danger! Warning!" about something currently in your life.

If this is so, what has God been speaking to you about in your life recently?"

_____
_____
_____

If this happened in the past and you were finally obedient to His Voice then write what it was, how you turned, and what impact it has had.

_____
_____
_____

## ...GAMES

6. "How great are His signs,
   And how mighty His wonders!
   His kingdom is an everlasting kingdom,
   And His dominion is from
   generation to generation."
   Daniel 4:3

At the top of page 156 I continue to share my musings by saying,

"He was able to positively identify 'it.' The 'thing' he'd met twice before when overdosing. The 'thing' that had ensnared him and continued living inside him. 'It,' 'she,' The 'thing' was an addiction. They had a love/hate relationship with Cody, and he with them. A Thug Life of their own.

Finally, the onlookers moved on. Cody believed in miracles but couldn't put a finger on whether or not he'd just been part of one. Signs from God. "What would it eventually take to beat my addiction? Without death or prison?"

You notice that in the tattoo shop while getting the "Thug Life" tattoo, I was certain that God was once again speaking to me, giving me a sign. I later found out that God has a wonderous way of speaking to us, and in a variety of ways. When He does speak to us, in whatever way He chooses, it certainly gives us the feeling that we're being communicated with by a higher power, God!

As you are beginning to open up to His Voice, you will find Him speaking to you through:

1. His Word (Scripture)

2. His Christian Fellowship (Christian One on Ones, Books, Music, etc.)

3. His Circumstance in your life (Godscidences: Providential and Perfectly timed events that you know could not happen outside of God.)

4. Prayer (Your Personal Communication through The Holy Spirit to God.)

Be sure to show up in every possible place He is speaking and be assured to hear His Voice for your life. Then be obedient to what you hear.

In the previous exercise, I asked you to identify how God was speaking to you specifically.

Now, answer these two questions in regard to what God is telling you about what you heard when you were listening.

What are three <u>short-term</u> goals to ensure that what God said to you will manifest itself in your life? (Weekly and or monthly)

1. _____
   _____
   _____

2. _____
   _____
   _____

3. _____
   _____
   _____

What are three <u>long-term</u> goals to ensure that what God said to you will manifest itself in your life? (Monthly and or Yearly)

1. _____
   _____
   _____

2. _____
   _____
   _____

3. _____
   _____
   _____

Way to go. This was a long day with a lot of tasks, but I assure you it is bearing much fruit for your life. Breathe and take it all in. This is what your delivered life will be like moving forward. I am very proud of you for all you have accomplished. God loves you in all you are and all you are doing.

Be sure to read Chapter 10 as you head into Day 14. See you soon.

# DAY 14

## CHAPTER 10

Welcome to Day 14! If you have re-read Chapter 10 then you can jump right into your daily prayer:

*"Dear Lord, I enter this prayer in the name of Your son Jesus Christ. I pray and thank You for allowing my faith in You to come alive in me as I continue through this 30-day program. I know that it is by faith that I continue forward, as I'm seeking something that sometimes feels impossible to conquer. By trusting You, I know that anything is possible including faith in being delivered from drugs and alcohol. Your word says, "For by Grace you have been saved through faith." Father, I believe that by my faith in You, You will deliver me. In Jesus Christ's name, Amen."*

Ok, now that you have been reminded that you have the Greatest on board (The Holy Spirit), continue on.

### THE CARDS TUMBLE...
### ...WITH RELEASE

1. In 2 Thessalonians 2:5-10 we find Paul saying, "Do you not remember that when I was still with you I told you these things? And now you know what is restraining, that he may be

revealed in his own time. For the mystery of lawlessness is already at work; only He who now restrains will do so until He is taken out of the way. And then the lawless one will be revealed, whom the Lord will consume with the breath of His mouth and destroy with the brightness of His coming. The coming of the lawless one is according to the working of Satan, with all power, signs, and lying wonders, and with all unrighteous deception among those who perish, because they did not receive the love of the truth, that they might be saved."

Now you find me speaking of myself on page 159 saying,

"Cody's buried addiction. It was all about to be brought into the light, and she knew it. It was horrifying at first. A pain that couldn't be readily subdued. All these emotions came crashing down like a wave on Cody's head. No shot of drugs to bury it. And all the while she stood there in her nakedness, ugly. The thing that had been trying to kill him, his addiction."

Maybe you can relate to what I wrote as you now partake in your 30-day program. When your addictions are brought to the light and revealed, it can be horrifying. There are "many emotions that come crashing down on your head," like the book reads, and many are hard to process. My prayer is that you never have to experience an intervention like I did with several police officers surrounding you. Regardless of the level of severity of your intervention, we've all had them prior to arriving right here.

Whether yours was personal, with family, and or with friends take a few moments to describe the emotions you felt when you were confronted with the thoughts of having to quit your addiction.

_____
_____
_____
_____
_____

Amazing your commitment to do the work. Way to go!

## …WITH RELIEF

2. Next, on page 164 you find the DEA agent taking the pictures of my tattoo's beginning to question me as to why I had decided to get such a ridiculous tattoo of "Thug Life." After reading that chapter, you are now a bit familiar with the "Thug Life" tattoo and why I got it. Yet, at that time however, the last thing I wanted to do was explain to a DEA officer why I had decided to get the tattoo. I simply said, "It's a long story."

With that in mind, it is now your opportunity to pick a tattoo on your body and explain "why" you got it. You've already done a similar exercise on a previous day, so pick a different tattoo for this one exercise. If you don't have a tattoo, pick a tattoo that you've thought about getting and write your "why" for wanting it and for not getting it. Or, if you have previously determined that your "Gateway Drug" was something other than tattoos, write out your "why" for that.

Here are some questions to guide you.

1. Why did you get or want to get the tattoo? What inspired it?
_____
_____
_____
_____

2. If you have a tattoo, how do you feel about it now?
_____
_____
_____
_____

3. If you didn't get the tattoo, why didn't you go through with it?
_____
_____
_____
_____

4. Why did you choose your "Gateway Drug"?
_____
_____
_____
_____

## ...WITH PAIN!

3. "So the great dragon was cast out, that serpent of old, called the Devil and Satan, who deceives the whole world; he was cast to the earth, and his angels were cast out with him." Revelation 12:9

On page 165 I speak of that very Devil when I say,
"That 'voice' manifested from lies Cody let himself believe as if true. She was born out of those lies. She thrived and grew from them. Now she was a gargantuan beast in full force exposing thoughts he

wanted to keep buried. They were the storms that collided to create her, the addiction."

If you are like me, you had or still have lies you let yourself believe to be true. One of the hardest things I ever had to do, was identify the lies that I constantly told myself, consistently letting the 'voice' speak as if they were true. Satan is the king of deception and lies, especially self-deception. He loves to prey on the weaknesses of men and woman. One of the most powerful and effective things you can ever do is identify the lies that Satan attempts to play on your mind. When they are exposed as lies, you see them at face value and for what they are worth, nothing.

At this point in your 30-day program you are ready to begin and identify the lies that Satan has told you were true in the past and the ones he is attempting to play on you right now.

Before you begin say this prayer:

*"In the name of Jesus Christ, I rebuke all satanic lies and deceptions. For Jesus Himself said, "Get behind me Satan! You are an offense to Me, for you are not mindful of the things of God, but the things of men." So, in the name of Jesus Christ, get behind me Satan. Jesus Christ defeated you 2,000 years ago and your "power" is a deception and a lie. Every thought of love is from God because God is love. Satan's lies and deceptions are not of love and not of God. I renounce them right now in the name of Jesus Christ. Reveal to me those lies and deceptions that are holding me in bondage or captive. Give me the courage to renounce each lie and deception as you reveal them to me. In Jesus Christ's name, Amen."*

Now, being reminded you have the Lord on Board, open your heart, mind, and spirit to identify and list as many lies that come to mind.

1. _____
   _____

2. _____
   _____

3. _____
   _____

4. _____
   _____

5. _____
   _____

(Go to your journal to continue and be ready as they are revealed.)

4. "Be strong and of good courage, do not fear nor be afraid of them; for the Lord your God, He is the One who goes with you. He will not leave you nor forsake you." Deuteronomy 31:6

Page 168 says,

"While he was wondering if the God he was reading about was watching over the void and darkness that he convinced himself he was in, Cody mumbling the words "I wonder if God's going to help me get through this?" Just then, Cody noticed something. He wasn't feeling pain from the lack of opiates in his system anymore, but he was starting to feel better, feel ok. He was sure it wasn't the voice telling him lies this time. Instead in his rock bottom condition, he was sure he heard something different. In the depths that he lay, he was certain he heard it. He hadn't heard it like this before, hadn't cared to. Through all the praying he had done when he was younger and at Boys Town, he hadn't heard it like this. He'd only claimed he had before, but now he was certain he "was." Two words he heard, no more, no less. Despite what Cody heard, he was struggling to accept it as true. Two words are all God said to him. "I'm here."

This was an extremely emotional point in my story, as I'm sure it is or will be for you and your story as well. Coming clean, and going through withdrawals, I came to the realization God had been with me all along. I hadn't allowed myself to accept help or love into my life, constantly drowning my feelings with drugs and attempting to bury them. Throughout the book you have found that I thought courage was something I personally needed to muster up myself, evident by the Chinese symbol that constantly resurfaced along with the thoughts of courage throughout the book. However, at the point in my story you just read, I realized that "He is the One who goes with you," just as the scripture above says. That, in and of itself, is where courage would derive from, God. He is the only one that can give us the courage we need to tackle obstacles. Humans are incapable of gaining the level of courage it's going to take to get through certain situations. When we trust and believe that God is right there with us, His strength in us fighting our toughest battles, what is there to ever fear? On that day I wrote about my position of rock bottom, I came to this realization that God was indeed with me. My prayer is that you too understand that God is right there with you. It will be helpful to read where Deuteronomy 31:6 says, "…He will not leave you, nor forsake you." Then continue to discover in your Bible where Galatians 4:6 and 2 Corinthians 1:22 says that He now resides in the presence of the Holy Spirit in your heart. This is the Spiritual Phenomenon of His word.

This knowledge and understanding are exactly what you need if you ever want to obtain and remain in sobriety. Deliverance from drugs and alcohol is not something human beings can achieve alone, but by God.

Take a moment and write out your answers to the following:

Do you believe that God is always with you? Then why or why not?

_____
_____
_____
_____
_____

Well, it has been another event filled day. You are just a day away from surpassing the halfway mark. Stay the course. Protect yourself from the lying voice of Satan who will begin to double down on you as he senses you reaching your understanding of "living delivered." Stay in the word and in fellowship with likeminded Christians.

I remain incredibly proud of you.

Once you have rested and internalized today get ready for Day 15 by re-reading Chapter 11. See you soon.

# DAY 15

## CHAPTER 11

Congratulations! You have arrived at Day 15. The actual halfway mark of your first 30 Days of your Life Delivered Program. Way to go! By now you probably don't even need reminding or prompting anymore for your daily prayer. It is a habit and I suspect one you will use to model any of your future endeavors.

*"Dear Lord, I enter this prayer in the name of Your son Jesus Christ. I pray and thank You for allowing my faith in You to come alive in me as I continue through this 30-day program. I know that it is by faith that I continue forward, as I'm seeking something that sometimes feels impossible to conquer. By trusting You, I know that anything is possible including faith in being delivered from drugs and alcohol. Your word says, "For by Grace you have been saved through faith." Father, I believe that by my faith in You, You will deliver me. In Jesus Christ's name, Amen."*

Hopefully, you feel primed and ready to dig in.

### 'COUNTY' A TASTE OF FREEDOM

1. "I closed my eyes and shook my head as I recalled the events of the last year. It was painful but not like the kind of pain getting tattoos had been. This was much different. A much more difficult

pain. The pain of the sudden realization of my wreckage," I wrote on page 169. In the beginning of this chapter, I came face to face with the realization of "my wreckage." My addiction. It was a very humbling moment. Though I'm not quite sure that "humbling" can fully describe it, if I was to pinpoint the very first step out of rock bottom that was necessary, I think this would be what was required. It became a massive step in the right direction towards the growth that would occur later on.

At this point in your 30-day program, I want you to think back and make a list of what you can identify as the "wreckage" you caused in your life by your addiction. Take your time and allow the Good Lord to open your eyes to be able to for now see clearly without harboring the pain the wreckage may have caused. (Number them if you separate them into different parts.)

_____
_____
_____
_____
_____

Do not delve into any systemic pain just yet. You will be handling that later. For now, keep moving forward.

2. I speak of my discovery on page 171 saying, "I didn't have much in the cell I could call my own. The few books were some of my only possessions. One of the books was the Bible I'd pulled from my nightstand; the one Father Peter had given me. Like the Tupac song, I'd found motivation in it. I knew I had not gone much further into it than the few sentences I'd read in my room the day I rediscovered

it. The day the DEA raided me. In fact, it had now become my 'lifeline.'"

During that time in County Jail, I leaned heavily on my Bible. Scripture became illuminated as I lay there, alone in my cell. Like I said in the book, it became my 'lifeline.' At this point in your 30-day program, it's time to see the Bible as your own lifeline. If you have just been reading the scriptures written in the Program, I am tasking you to find your own Bible, your own lifeline. There are a number of ways to obtain one in today's world. When you have a Bible in hand, search within its pages and identify a scripture that speaks to you. You may have already had one God is pointing you to from the ones in the program and that will be ok for now. Yet, sooner or later, you will find the Holy Spirit pointing toward a special one of your very own to stand on. This "pointing" by God through the Holy Spirit I also refer to, from time to time, as "pricking."

However, you happen to come upon your scripture, take some time to write it out below. Then, add a description as to why you chose that specific scripture and how it is speaking to you personally.

Scripture:_____

_____
_____
_____
_____
_____

Why & How:

_____
_____
_____
_____
_____

(I recommend reciting throughout your day until you own it personally)

3. Now, I continue on page 171 saying,

"I had been forced to do something I hadn't done in a very long time, confront myself. I had attended Narcotics Anonymous once a week in my jail pod. I'd been introduced to a word I'd heard before but had never dreamed about calling myself, addict. "Hi, my names Cody and I'm an addict," I'd said it because I felt I had to. Everyone else was, so I fell in line with the others. Only later, alone in my cell did I process the claim and attempt to understand it's complexity. "Hi, my name is Cody and I'm an addict," I'd said it to myself in the very mirror I was currently looking into while cutting my hair. This new title I'd given myself, I wanted to know what it meant to be an addict. "Why am I an addict?" This question I couldn't answer. Not even with the help of my Bible."

One of the main differences between learning to live as an addict of most 12-step programs and actually being delivered from addiction by Jesus Christ, is that we no longer have to identify as being an addict, because when delivered, you're not one. You were one, but you are no longer one. In Jesus Christ, God has brought you to the very point in your life BEFORE drugs were ever introduced into it.

Referring to the scripture from 1 John 1:9: "If we confess our sins, He is faithful and just to forgive us our sins and to cleanse us from *all* unrighteousness." The Bible doesn't say He will cleanse us from a little bit of unrighteousness. Or perhaps some unrighteousness, but rather, *all* unrighteousness. Yes, including the transgression of addiction.

Because I believe every word written in the Holy Bible and I believe those words to be The Truth, I believe that when I confessed my sins of addiction to Jesus Christ, I was no longer bound to the identification of being called an addict. This is not only a pillar of this program, but more importantly it is a pillar of Christianity.

The same position of deliverance became yours when you surrendered your addiction to God through Jesus Christ. It is time for you to receive, accept, and engage the vision He has for you.

Follow this exercise to help reveal how you currently feel He is calling you to see yourself. Put your name in the first spaces, and in the second, put anything you are, other than an addict. Ready…Go!!

Hi, My name is_____ and
I'm_____.

Hi, My name is_____ and
I'm_____.

Hi, My name is_____ and
I'm_____.

Hi, My name is_____ and
I'm_____.

That was pretty powerful, wasn't it? Are you beginning to see what it is to be in God's Love? That is my hope and prayer for you.

4. On page 176 you will find that I read a note to the courtroom and to my family and friends. It was an apology mixed with a plea of forgiveness from my friends and family. This, I later learned, is *Intellectually reasoned forgiveness.* Simply put, this is forgiveness without the specific presence of God. Or put another way, forgiveness without the involvement of God. Forgiveness itself is defined as the letting go of sin. In the Bible, this includes forgiving everyone, every time, of everything, as an act of obedience and gratefulness to God. Therefore, the chapter is titled: County A Taste of Freedom. The "taste of freedom" in the chapter's title is that very intellectually reasoned forgiveness. Unfortunately, this is not the forgiveness that gets you to the prize of being delivered from addiction. However, don't get me wrong my friend, it is a good steppingstone in the right direction. Clearly a steppingstone that I used and quite possibly you used as well.

The actual *deliverance forgiveness* necessary, (Spiritually Graced) was touched on during a previous day of the program. I assure you it will be expounded upon later. For now, though, using the *Intellectually reasoned forgiveness,* I'd like you to write a letter of forgiveness to your friends and/or family, just like I did that day in the courtroom. No need for perfection for your "Taste of Freedom."

Dear_____

_____
_____
_____
_____
_____
_____
_____
_____
_____
_____
_____
_____
_____
_____
_____
_____
_____
_____
_____
_____

Sincerely_____

Wow! You continue to make me proud with your engagement of the exercises, assignments, and questions. Take it all in my friend. You are growing mightily.

Be sure to re-read Chapter 12 and I will see you again at Day 16.

# DAY 16

## CHAPTER 12

Ok, on to Day 16, the second half of your first 30 Days To Life Deliverance Program. Get ready to come alive from the foundation you just built in the first fifteen days. Let's Go!

*"Dear Lord, I enter this prayer in the name of Your son Jesus Christ. I pray and thank You for allowing my faith in You to come alive in me as I continue through this 30-day program. I know that it is by faith that I continue forward, as I'm seeking something that sometimes feels impossible to conquer. By trusting You, I know that anything is possible including faith in being delivered from drugs and alcohol. Your word says, "For by Grace you have been saved through faith." Father, I believe that by my faith in You, You will deliver me. In Jesus Christ's name, Amen."*

Now being reminded you have the Lord on Board, with Chapter 12 having been read, and your Bible in hand it is time to jump in.

## 'FEDERAL' A TASTE OF DIRECTION

1. "But He said to them, "Why are you fearful, O you of little faith?" Then He arose and rebuked the winds and the sea, and there was a great calm."   Matthew 8:26

I continue my story on pages 181 & 182 saying,

"A new rock bottom had been found. One I thought couldn't get much deeper after the DEA had confronted me that day in the gym. I had been wrong though and was now discovering that the rock bottom is relative and going deeper can always be found, no matter where I am, including Leavenworth. As I stood there in thought, sulking, and questioning how I ended up in Leavenworth the holding cell door opened. An officer took one step into the room and barked an order "I need inmate Lanus, 17632030."

This was a point in my journey where I could confidently say, "God had His hand over my life." Just when I thought I was going to be going deep into one of the most infamous prisons in the country, Leavenworth, God reached down and pulled me out of that potentially very terrible situation. I can hear Jesus now, "Why are you fearful, O you of little faith?" I had been indeed guilty of having very little faith, like that of a mustard seed little, yet God still stepped in to rebuke the winds and the seas in my life.

It's amazing how when you're fighting your toughest battles, God always shows up to give you the breath of fresh air you were needing. Even if I would have entered into Leavenworth, I now know at this point that God would still have had His hand of protection over my life. It's this understanding of God and Faith that allows us our confidence and peace.

Take a moment and look back at a situation in your life that you thought couldn't get any worse, yet God showed up at that very moment to rebuke the winds and the sea in your situation. Then write it down and explain how in hindsight you discovered it was His Hand at work.

_____

_____

_____

Pretty amazing, isn't He? Can you begin to see the promise of your future in Him?

2. "For you see your calling, brethren, that not many wise according to the flesh, not many mighty, not many noble, are called. But God has chosen the foolish things of the world to put to shame the wise, and God has chosen the weak things of the world to put to shame the things which are mighty; and the base things of the world and the things which are despised God has chosen, and the things which are not, to bring to nothing the things that are, that no flesh should glory in His presence."   1 Corinthians 1:26-29

On page 186 I share a mother's plea saying,

"Tears formed in the woman's eyes. She pulled her red hair behind her ear with one hand and wiped the falling tear with the other. The Camp Driver and I looked on at the scene unfolding, not exactly sure how we should respond. Frozen we waited. "My son overdosed last month and is in outpatient rehab. He works in this hospital," she finally said through tears. She grabbed my hand and looked me in the eyes. The tears continuing to well. "Do you think you could talk to him?" she asked."

This was the first time I had someone approach me to possibly help them through a situation of despair. I never thought, at that time in my own despair, anyone cared to get help from somebody like me, a recovering addict, inmate. God works in unique ways though. God uses the ordinary to achieve the extraordinary. If you don't think God is about to call on you for something amazing, I'm here to tell you you're wrong. I don't know the exact time, place, or call, but I do know that you have exactly what God is looking for: "the base things of the world and the things which are despised God has chosen, and the things which are not, to bring to nothing the things that are," as the scripture above reads.

As for now, at this stage of the Program, I am going to task you to reach out and help someone you know, that is struggling with any type of bondage or addiction. You are ready to begin being the light for someone. Pray on it, asking God to open your heart to who this person is. Then, act, text, email, or call them and set up a time to talk with them about something amazing. Or, if you're in prison or jail yourself, God will prick you to approach someone you hang out with. In either case, invite them to read TATTOOS and invite them to join the 30 Days To Life Program. Tell them your story to this point and let them see, feel, and hear what God has done for you.

You may feel like you're not ready to help anyone, just as I was that day in the hospital talking to the nurse. I'm not asking you to push anything down their throat or make them do something they don't want to. I'm respectfully asking you to invite someone suffering with an addiction to experience some love.

The fact is that it is not you, me, the book, or the Program that works in the spirit of a person to move, it is God, so remember to pray before you set out on this courageous journey:

"Dear Jesus, I ask for Your strength and courage as I go forward on this journey. I ask you to let the Holy Spirit be illuminated through me to guide my words and actions as I speak with the one You call me to who is suffering with an addiction. Jesus, lift me up to become exactly what you've called me to be, despite what I think I am incapable of being. With You Jesus, anything is possible, and no task is too great. For if You are with me, who can possibly be against me. In Jesus Christ's name I pray, Amen."

Without using the person's real name here be sure to come back and write out your outreach and how you feel it went.

_____
_____
_____

I am very proud of you for being obedient to God's call.

3. You will find me saying on page 190, "This wasn't the condition a mother should see her son in. A pain ached within me, a pain signaling I didn't want food. I stepped out of the line and headed back to my unit to lay on my bunk. For the first time since college had ended, I picked up a pen and began journaling. I poured my feelings onto paper in my new home. It had sparked feelings within me."

When I finally got settled into prison, one of the things that helped me relieve stress, was journaling. I'd write and write, sometimes staying up late into the night. It was like the paper was the one thing that would listen to me (This was before I learned the power of prayer and meditating on God's Word. However, at that time in my walk with God, just journaling itself was very therapeutic). I felt I had nobody to express my feelings to inside the walls of prison, but the paper seemed to always be listening, and it still does. I often still find myself filling notepads with randomly chosen topics or thoughts. Then again, was it actually God's hand in that randomness as well?

Being amazed at how fast I was able to load up a journal, I can begin to understand why Paul was able to write four books of the New Testament during his own incarceration, and why those words within those books are so moving. Being confined coupled with the raw emotions, seems to open the mind up for God inspired writings.

If you have not already done *more* than use your journal as an overflow for your Program questions, then this is your opportunity to do so. To start journaling your thoughts, experiences, emotions, and the like, on a topic that moves you. If you are not moved, then get with God in prayer and see what topic He points you to. Then be obedient and journal.

If you are more like me, then you are finding yourself at a point in your life where you'd like to fully express your thoughts and emotions somewhere. Your journal is just the place. You will also find that down the road your written words will be highly valuable to you as well. There are no boundaries or restrictions. Just pour your emotions onto the paper.

Ready....Go!

When you have finished this journaling exercise be sure to re-read Chapter 13 in preparation for Day 17. See you soon.

# DAY 17

## CHAPTER 13

You are on the move again into Day 17. I trust you found some real emotional feeling of growth as you accomplished the last task. Now, having re-read Chapter 13, you can begin today with the prayer:

*"Dear Lord, I enter this prayer in the name of Your son Jesus Christ. I pray and thank You for allowing my faith in You to come alive in me as I continue through this 30-day program. I know that it is by faith that I continue forward, as I'm seeking something that sometimes feels impossible to conquer. By trusting You, I know that anything is possible including faith in being delivered from drugs and alcohol. Your word says, "For by Grace you have been saved through faith." Father, I believe that by my faith in You, You will deliver me. In Jesus Christ's name, Amen."*

Get ready to see yourself even more inside this Day.

## THE STORY OF THE ROSE...
## BEGINS IN CONFRONTATION...

1. "And not only that, but we also glory in tribulations, knowing that tribulation produces perseverance; and perseverance, character; and character, hope. Now hope does not disappoint, because

the love of God has been poured out in our hearts by the Holy Spirit who was given to us." Romans 5:3-5

Reading from the Book on page 194 I mention my initial confrontation with the Old Man saying, "Before I could reach him on the other side of the kitchen, he had been confronted by another kitchen worker. Another *Bible Beater*. Not to be told about the rules, however, they were both discussing religion. Apparently, they both attended church together. I listened in as the words of "Christianity", "God", and "Jesus" were tossed around. I laughed as I folded my hands to my chest. "Inmate Christians," I pondered. The hypocrisy amusing. "Never trust an inmate Jesus Freak." As I pretended to occupy myself, I listened to their conversation and thought of Kayli.

I remember that day in the kitchen, before rededicating my born-again life, and scoffing at Gary (The Old Man) and the inmate he was talking to. It upset me that these two were laughing and joking yet living in such a terrible place like prison. Simply put, I was upset at their joy. "How could they be so happy in such an unhappy place?" I remember thinking to myself. Like the scripture above says, and like these two Christians clearly understood, their current tribulation would eventually produce hope if it hadn't already.

"Hope does not disappoint," as the scripture says. Why? Because this is how we find God's love. In these trying times, we can discover just how much God actually loves us, if we so choose to search Him out. Of course, at the moment in the kitchen I was witnessing their joy, I took it as something much different. Deep down though, I wanted that joy more than anything. Something within me convicted me on that day. I knew that if I was to obtain this kind of Peace, Joy, and Love, I was going to have to really search out this Jesus guy. In the previous chapter I had acquired all these *self-help* books, including a Bible. I was sensing that it was the time to really start reading the Bible if I was going to find my answers. Now it is your turn as well.

Earlier in the 30-day program I had tasked you with obtaining a Bible. Trusting you have done that and found your way around it a bit, I'd like you to pause right now and go to your Bible. Now search it to find three scriptures that speak to you regarding Hope, Peace, or Love. Then answer, "Why do these scriptures speak to you?" Call on the Holy Spirit to Guide you, to be your GPS navigator!

1. Hope_____
_____
_____

2. Peace_____
_____
_____

3. Love_____
_____
_____

2. "And Jesus rebuked the demon, and it came out of him; and the child was cured from that very hour," Matthew 17:18

I continue to speak of Kayli on page 195 saying, "She'd succumbed to a hideous demon, depression. A demon I'd recognized. A demon I was still fighting while locked up in prison. I had questions, none of which this "God" or "Jesus" character had ever answered. Seething for answers it was time to approach this old man who'd wandered into my kitchen, who'd brought these feelings erupting to the surface with his Jesus talk?"

Growing up Catholic, I was taught that if you take your own life, you go to hell. Obviously, on this day, I was wrestling with both Kayli's death and where she would spend eternity based on what I was taught earlier in my life. Why I challenged Gary on that day to answer such a difficult question, was beyond me. Mostly, I was frustrated. Frustrated with my situation and frustrated with God. Looking back now, I can see that this was actually a good thing. Why? Because when you find yourself frustrated at God, and searching for His answers, it means you believe in Him. It means you actually do have Faith. Obviously, I didn't realize that back then, but looking back on it now, I can see this as an incremental point in my relationship *back* to Christ, being angry at Him.

Pause for a moment and ponder this. Then write it out.

Are you finding yourself "angry" at God?

\_\_\_\_ Yes \_\_\_\_ No

In either answer explain why?

_____

_____

_____

_____

Proud of you for being direct. God hears you and is working within you right now to rectify or support your position with Him. Be at the very Peace you looked up earlier and let Him do what He does best!

3. "And the prayer of the faith will save the sick, and the Lord will raise him up. And if he has committed sins, he will be forgiven. Confess your trespasses to one another, and pray for one another, that you may be healed. The effective, fervent prayer of a righteous man avails much." James 5:15-16

As you can see on page 195, I was ready for the old man, saying,

"I hit him with it, a sucker punch I knew he wouldn't expect. I was never one to hide the words I felt, and this man was about to experience it firsthand. "I had a good friend just commit suicide. Where is she, Heaven, or Hell?" I bellowed at him."

If you're a parent, the last thing you would ever want your child to do, is take their life to get out of a problem. God feels the same way. We are called children of God when we place our faith in His son Jesus Christ who died on the cross for our sins. The last thing God ever wants, is for someone to take their own life as a means to an end of a problem. God wants them to lean on Him to get through any and all obstacles. When Satan and his devils, demons, minions, fiends, or imps conspire to take a life, and succeed in moving a person to do so, that doesn't mean God sends them to hell. If their faith was placed in Jesus Christ, it means they're forgiven, just as the scripture above says. We must remember that in most cases we are not given the insight of another person as to the day, the hour, the second, or the microsecond they may have called upon the Lord Jesus Christ for freedom and salvation from their plight of life. These are things of God and not of man. Yet, our hope, prayer, faith, and trust are that all of our loved ones, in whatever manner they leave us, were afforded the opportunity to do so at one time and seized upon it.

We do know full well that when we do meet them in Heaven, they would have surely had that beautiful, wonderful, encounter of the Heart with Jesus Christ while here. This, God calls us to be at Peace with Him and use that Peace to keep moving to be the light for others that He is in us.

Gary, in all his wisdom and knowledge, enlightened me on this fact on that day. What a blessed, Holy Spirit filled day we had in the prison's kitchen of all places.

Is Satan or his devils, demons, minions, fiends, or imps filling your head with lies, allowing depression and gloom to creep in?

Pause and think on that question. Then take this time to write the lies down in preparation to renounce them.

_____
_____
_____
_____
_____

Now, confess any and all of those negative thoughts and lies from the enemy that you feel are holding you bondage and renounce them with this prayer:

*"Dear God, In the name of Jesus Christ my Lord, I come to you with this prayer for release. In Name of Jesus Christ, I renounce you Satan and all your lies and deceptions used to try and defeat me. I now pray*

*that You Lord will expose any lies of Satan I have believed and allow Your Holy Spirits Peace, Hope, and Joy to now fill my heart and mind. Father God, I know that You are all mighty and powerful and stronger that any of these lies that Satan has used to play on my mind. You created the Heavens and the Earth, and You create Happiness within me, because You created me. Thank You for continuing to overflow my soul with Your Holy Spirit Love, letting it flood over my body. Let nothing but truth and light shine through me and fill any void that darkness may try to exist in. All this I pray, in Jesus Christ's name, Amen"*

Wow! Have you just felt the weight lift from your shoulders, your mind, your spirit? Remember to return to this type of reflection, confession, and renounce Satan's lies in the name of Jesus' Christ as often as you feel the enemy creating pressure within you.

You have once again done a great job engaging. Practice, Practice, Practice!

Be sure to be prepared to wrap up Chapter 13 by re-reading it prior to Day 18.

See you there soon.

# DAY 18

## CHAPTER 13

You are ready to wrap up Chapter 13 on Day 18. You did a great job engaging once again in some very personal areas on the previous day. You will grow today as well. Time for your daily prayer:

"Dear Lord, I enter this prayer in the name of Your son Jesus Christ. I pray and thank You for allowing my faith in You to come alive in me as I continue through this 30-day program. I know that it is by faith that I continue forward, as I'm seeking something that sometimes feels impossible to conquer. By trusting You, I know that anything is possible including faith in being delivered from drugs and alcohol. Your word says, "For by Grace you have been saved through faith." Father, I believe that by my faith in You, You will deliver me. In Jesus Christ's name, Amen."

Here you go.

## THE STORY OF THE ROSE…
## …YET PROGRESSES

1. "And we know that all things work together for good to those who love God, to those who are the called according to His purpose. For whom He foreknew, He also predestined to be con-

formed to the image of His Son, that He might be the firstborn among many brethren. Moreover whom He predestined, these He also called, whom He called, these he also justified; and whom He justified, these He also glorified." Romans 8:28-30

On page 196 and 197 you find me speaking of Gary by saying, "He pushed the paper away and once again made eye contact as he had in the kitchen. "Kayli's a ten, you're a ten, we're all tens," he continued. "In God's eyes we're not a seed or a rose bush. It doesn't matter the stage of life you're in. We're all the same to God. Absolute tens," he (*Gary*) finished.

If you're ever questioning your worth, like I had many times in my addictions, just take a good look at a picture of Jesus Christ on the cross. If you believe that Jesus Christ went to that cross, died for your sins, rose from the dead, and ascended into Heaven to be seated at the right hand of the Father, then you have been made more than worthy "In Christ." As a matter of fact, you've been "justified" (made right). You are glorified! God no longer looks at your sin. He looks and sees you through His Son Jesus Christ. Why? Because He died on the cross and took that burden for mankind so you could have a relationship with His Father. You are now very worthy in God's eyes, and despite what you might sometimes call yourself when you feel down, you are a child of the Most High God! And, despite how Kayli died, she too is still a child of God, and a perfect 10!

Today in your 30-day program, I challenge you to make five posts on social media simply telling someone something positive about themselves that you see or feel about them. If you don't have social media, simply text, email, or send a letter to those five people. Get with God as to who they may be and let Him Guide you into the best way to let them know they are the *Rose*; they are a 10. Write out the names of the five names with a short snapshot of what you shared with them.

1._____
_____
_____

2._____
_____
_____

3._____
_____
_____

4._____
_____
_____

5._____
_____
_____

Way to go! Can you feel the peace that comes with such sharing?

2. "…If anyone thirsts, let him come to Me and drink. He who believes in Me, as the Scriptures has said, out of his heart will flow rivers of living water." John 7:37-38

Now on page 197 Gary continues saying,

"When you stop trying to *be something* you already are and when you stop trying to *find something* you already have, your life will change." Gary said this as he pointed to my chest, toward my heart.

I now understand what Gary was talking about when he pointed to my chest, and towards my heart. He was referring to the Holy Spirit that lives inside me, God's Helper to all of us who believe. "Out of his heart will flow rivers of living water," the Scripture above reads. How amazing to know that when you placed your faith in Jesus Christ, God's Holy Spirit, was given to you to live within your heart forever. Go to Galatians 4:6 and 2 Corinthians 1:22 to hear it directly from Paul.

As a believer in Jesus Christ, you don't need to try and be something society claims you need to be, as you already are what God called you to be. You have the gift of the Holy Spirit that dwells within you: Guiding, leading, and directing you every step of the way. Many people suffering from drug and/or alcohol abuse, use these substances to make themselves feel good or feel high. I'm here to tell you that the same God that created the Universe, conceived Jesus in Mary's womb, and raised Jesus from the dead, also lives within us who believe in Jesus Christ. Knowing the power that lives within you, gives you a greater high than drugs or alcohol ever could, and it's the same power that delivers you from your addictions as well. The more you know, understand, embrace, and engage this truth, the stronger your life's walk will become.

You have been asked to be a part of prayer many times throughout this 30-day program and I am proud of you for always stepping in to do so. Now, I want to task you to create a personal prayer for yourself. In it find your own voice, your own language to ask God,

## DAY 18

through Jesus Christ, what it is exactly that you're searching for. Then, recite it out loud to yourself even if it is just above a whisper. Continue by meditating on God's word that has been given to you. Finally, write down what God is telling you in answer to that prayer.

Remember to show up in the four places where He speaks (Word, Witness, Godscidences, & Prayer) so as not to miss His Voice.

Enjoy your time with God.

Prayer:

_____
_____
_____
_____
_____

His Voice:

_____
_____
_____
_____
_____

Alright my friend. What and accomplishment. Let this be the beginning of your new habit in prayer language guided by the Holy Spirit in you.

You are now ready for *The Calling*… be sure to re-read Chapter 14 and I will see you again at Day 19!

# DAY 19

## CHAPTER 14

Welcome to Day 19. Trusting you have re-read Chapter 14 you are ready to continue your growth in this amazing journey. Once again begin with your daily prayer:

*"Dear Lord, I enter this prayer in the name of Your son Jesus Christ. I pray and thank You for allowing my faith in You to come alive in me as I continue through this 30-day program. I know that it is by faith that I continue forward, as I'm seeking something that sometimes feels impossible to conquer. By trusting You, I know that anything is possible including faith in being delivered from drugs and alcohol. Your word says, "For by Grace you have been saved through faith." Father, I believe that by my faith in You, You will deliver me. In Jesus Christ's name, Amen."*

Now, fully armed, dig right in!

### THE CALLING...

1. "Wait on the Lord;
   Be of good courage,
   And he shall strengthen you heart;
   Wait, I say, on the Lord!"
   Psalm 27:14

On page 199 you hear my reaction to fellow inmate Paul when he kept after me to write my story of spiraling into addiction saying,

"You have got to be kidding me, Paul. That is the most ridiculous thing I've ever heard. A fentanyl dealer? A freaking fentanyl dealer? I'm the last person Trump would pardon."

As a society in general most of us, despite our level of faith, rely on man. We get upset when things don't go our way, and we get even more upset when things don't happen when we want them to. I can honestly say, that one of the greatest things that has happened to me since placing my faith in Jesus Christ, is that I've obtained real patience and real peace. Throughout my entire life I had been trying to fit a square peg into a round hole, getting upset when things didn't go my way. I had, instead of waiting on the Lord, placed my faith in man.

(Take a moment and go read Galatians 4:4-7 again to lock in the understanding of the *real* peace I am talking about and the way to receive it.)

What I found out was that when you place your faith in man, you quite often are let down. See, while you were once suffering from drug addiction, this often seemed to cause you to spiral into using drugs on many different occasions to soften the pain of the letdown. The downward spiral continued, right? Well, now as you choose to go to the Lord, wait on the Lord and stay faithful in prayer to the Lord, you will gain an understanding of what God's will is for your life and your choices within it. You will find that His Will occurs in His capacity for you and when He sees it fit to bring it about. (Remember what you learned of patience having its perfect work?

Well, this is it!) And when it occurs and you are obedient to it you will then find that the square peg now becomes a round peg, and everything fits perfectly into the round hole. There will be no frustration or anxiety, no longer the sting of let downs and disappointments by man. When you wait on the Lord, you get 100% of what you seek, 100% of the time, all in accordance with God's Will for our lives. Sometimes it's necessary to tell your own children no because you know that they just aren't ready for it. The same happens with you and God. Take me for example, I now believe wholeheartedly that God knows when I'll be released from prison. Not Trump! Not Biden! Not the Warden! Not a Judge! But God!

What are you placing your faith in and relying on today?

\_\_\_\_ God? \_\_\_\_ Man? \_\_\_\_ Both?

Does your response seem to spring from the remnant of your addictive tendencies or from your newfound Faith in God, through Jesus Christ, and the Holy Spirit in your heart?

Take a moment and write your answer, including exactly what was going through your mind as you were posed those questions. Your spirit was pricked in pondering them. Get your thoughts out on paper so as to let them be a litmus test for your growth in the Program.

_____
_____
_____
_____

Book mark this page and come back to it to experience your progress.

2. "For the gifts and the calling of God are irrevocable." Romans 11:29

Gary shares and I react on page 203 and 204 saying,

"See Cody, when I am released, I am called to put together a company that will from time-to-time feature books that I believe will have an impact on people's lives physically, mentally, emotionally, and spiritually. I have been studying and listening to stories over the last 6 years in prison of the many reasons surrounding why men get tattoos. I believe there is an element of it that is not being exposed in a single tattoo event. Yet, it can be revealed by hearing of how they evolve, over time, within a man's mind and on his body. I would like that hidden element to be exposed and feature it as one of the books someday. I know this is a lot to ask and I just jumped you with it, so take some time and think about if you would like to even write about your tattoo experiences. "Why me?" I snapped a bit puzzled.

How many times have you said, "Why me?" Most the time I find that we say, "Why me?" to the negative things that happen in our life. We surely aren't asking God the question at that moment. We say, "Why me?" to ourselves as if we will be able to explain the Divine intervention that's occurred. But let's focus on the "good" things that happen in our lives: a newborn baby, a wonderful marriage, or perhaps a new home or car you were suddenly able to afford. We often ask ourselves, "Why me?" in the face of these blessings. For me, it was this opportunity to use the relationship with Gary to create a product to help people suffering from addiction, just as I was being called to do that day. "Why me?" Furthermore, how many of us find self-destruction in response to amazing opportunities, denying God's calling for us? It's often said that most of us

## DAY 19

are more afraid of success than we are of failure. This is true because we have been taught to fear failure, when in fact success is actually achieved through a series of failures. Those that understand that go on to succeed. Those that don't, which is most, do not succeed. Most see successful people on T.V. or social media and say, "How did they get so lucky?" "How did they stumble on to the perfect opportunity?" In reality, if you look back on all the opportunities in life you turned down saying with doubt, "Why me?", you'd discover that maybe you'd have been just as successful if you would have first got with God and let Him Guide you. Then when the yes came you would find yourself saying "Thank you God!" instead. You'd be more successful that even your wildest dreams could have predicted. Well, that was then, and this is now. No turning back for a do-over of past events. Only what God is laying before the new "In Christ" you. Time to rethink, refocus, rediscover, reconnect and reach out when opportunity arises. He knows.

Let's see where you currently let your mind go.

What are you currently saying, "Why me?" about in your life?

_____
_____
_____
_____

What action will you take to find out what you should do?

_____
_____
_____
_____

Way to go once again. Mind and Sprit working hard in you!

3. Rejoice always, pray without ceasing, in everything give thanks, For this is the will of God in Christ Jesus for you."

1 Thessalonians 5:16-18

On page 205 I reveal what came next by saying,

"I began meeting with Gary over the book he believed so dearly in. From weekly to daily to many times during a single day we met. The discovery of my voice in the stories surrounding each tattoo and of my journey into the world of drugs and addiction in between them was now driving me to the same belief. Then one day Gary asked out of the blue as he sat facing me across the ice room, "Cody, have you discovered the "antidote" to your drug addiction within your stories yet? The real lasting NARCAN of addiction?"

These meetings with Gary were powerful, life-changing in many ways. We'd always start and end these meetings with prayer, or rather, Gary would pray. At first, like many babes in Christ, I felt awkward praying. Therefore, I was never the one praying. Eventually though, that would change. To this day my prayer life continues to grow. From these awkward prayers, grew my current prayer life. I now find myself leading prayers here in prison during church service, praying after workouts, praying before meals, praying on the phone, praying before bed. There isn't ever a bad time to pray. These meetings with Gary would mark the beginning of my relationship back to Christ, through prayer. And not only that, through prayer I found myself eventually able to answer this challenging question that Gary often presented to me: "Cody, have you discovered the "antidote" to your drug addiction within your stories yet? The real lasting NARCAN of addiction?" Now it's time for you to delve in to answering the question.

"Have you discovered the "antidote" to your drug addiction within your stories yet? The real lasting NARCAN of addiction?"

Write out what you believe to this point in the program the "antidote" is.

This is not a test question but a journey question, no right or wrong at this point, just current understanding of it written down. Go for it!

_____
_____
_____
_____

4. "For you were once darkness, but now you are light in the Lord. Walk as children of light (for the fruit of the Spirit is in all goodness, righteousness, and truth), finding out what is acceptable to the Lord. And have no fellowship with the unfruitful works of darkness, but rather expose them." Ephesians 5:8-11

Gary taught me that sometimes it's best to learn things the hard way, by discovering it yourself rather than being given the answer the easy way. I certainly fought against this and often found myself very frustrated. "What is the Antidote?" I'd say to myself in my cell. Sometimes I'd even convince myself it didn't exist. Then, as my prayer life grew, so my relationship with God also grew. Then, God revealed certain things to me over time. What was once darkness, became illuminated. "For you were once darkness, but now you are light in the Lord," as the scripture above says. I started to see who I was, why I was in the position I was in, and most importantly, where I was going. Answering these questions about myself, allowed me to "have no fellowship with unfruitful works of darkness, but rather expose them," once again as the scripture above says. Here is an opportunity in your 30-day program to answer these questions yourself.

Remember these are journey questions. Like me, you will find the answer to these three questions continuing to evolve as you also grow in your prayer life and your relationship with God. But for now, let's hear what you currently think.

1. Who are you?

_____
_____
_____

2. Why are you in the position you're in?

_____
_____
_____

3. Where are you going?

_____
_____
_____

Proud of you once again. Keep on keeping on with your journey. God is working mightily in you. Be sure to read Chapter 15 before jumping into Day 20. I'll see you there.

# DAY 20

## CHAPTER 15

You have now arrived at Day 20! I trust you are feeling the growth in your Deliverance Journey. Now that you have re-read Chapter 15 let's dig in. You know where to start, right?

*"Dear Lord, I enter this prayer in the name of Your son Jesus Christ. I pray and thank You for allowing my faith in You to come alive in me as I continue through this 30-day program. I know that it is by faith that I continue forward, as I'm seeking something that sometimes feels impossible to conquer. By trusting You, I know that anything is possible including faith in being delivered from drugs and alcohol. Your word says, "For by Grace you have been saved through faith." Father, I believe that by my faith in You, You will deliver me. In Jesus Christ's name, Amen."*

Now, being reminded that you have the Lord on Board, let's go.

## THE LOGAN EFFECT
## COINCIDENCE...

1. "Let all bitterness, wrath, anger, clamor, and evil speaking be put away from you, with all malice. And be kind to one another, tender-

hearted, forgiving one another, even as God in Christ forgave you." Ephesians 4:31-32

On page 210 I reveal my emotion saying, "This feeling I had as I got 'angry' began circulating in my stomach. I attempted to subdue it with positive self-talk and positive imagery. The very self-control strategies I'd relied on time and time again. Then I slipped. "Why couldn't they just unlock the doors on time?" I thought to myself. "Why the hell is everything such a pain in the ass around here?"

On that day, I was clearly struggling. I can recall similar situations, before being incarcerated, when anger led to drug use on several occasions. In prison however, I was left to *handle* the situation, rather than avoid it by getting high. I found that anger is a ruthless emotion that never meshes well in the lives of those suffering with addictions. Anger was often the catalyst to voids being filled. Simply put: Anger often contributed to my mental deterioration, magnifying the things that often caused much of my drug use. For some reason, when I became angry, it seemed to bring up the memory of *ALL* the things I was ever angry about. Then, like a gust of wind picking up speed, it would soon be that within me. I remember using this superpower of anger to physically accomplish many great things in my life. But it also became my Achilles heel, ultimately leading to my downfall and incarceration.

So, is there a solution? If so, then what is it?

Is there a cure? If so, what is it?

It was revealed to Paul almost 2,000 years ago and he laid it out perfectly in the Scripture above from Ephesians: "And be kind to one another, tender hearted, forgiving one another, even as God in Christ forgave you!"

Take a moment and write down some situations that seem to cause you, or have caused you in the past to become angry?

_____
_____
_____
_____
_____

Also, related to that anger, write out who you feel it's time to forgive?

_____
_____
_____
_____
_____

Be sure to make a note moving forward every time anger flares up and write it out and see if you can determine who or what needs to be forgiven. Forgiveness itself is defined as the letting go of sin. In the Bible, this includes forgiving everyone, every time, of everything, as an act of obedience and appreciation to God. It acknowledges the sacrifice God made through His Son Jesus who died to restore the relationship between God and you.

2. "But Jesus looked at them and said to them, "With men this is impossible, but with God all things are possible." Matthew 19:26

This surfaces for me, where I continue reading Gary's letter, on page 212,

"All things are possible with God. Go to Him for strength and guidance in that path. He will not let you down. You are a Holy Spirit filled man and you can control the height of its flame in your heart. It is at the calling of your voice. Mastering that and its power to fulfill your life will astonish you. I have great faith in you because I know God's got you. We really perform our best when we perform for the audience of "One."

Clearly, in that first sentence of Gary's letter to me, he was utilizing what Jesus spoke in Matthew's Gospel. I was thinking maybe, just maybe, Gary was talking about conquering my addiction as the *possible* with God thing.

To believe that *all* things are possible with God, is to take God at His Word. To take God at His word, is to have faith. This is not always easy, especially when things don't go like we want them to. Within life's financial burdens, sickness and deaths, marriage, and relationship problems, and even addictions, we all have hurdles that present themselves from time to time. Believing that God can bring us through them is when we "perform at our best" as Gary said in his letter to me. My hope and belief are that most want to perform at their best. If that is you, then to do just that you will need to remember that God is always in control. He orchestrates or allows events to be. He hardens and softens hearts. He binds and loosens minds. He does this during what we see as the good times and the bad times. Knowing and Trusting in God, we need to remain faithful that He will bring us through. Pause and say this prayer of faith:

*"Dear God, Lord Jesus Christ, I know that with You, all things are possible. No addiction stands a chance as I stand In Christ Jesus. I believe that with You as my Advocate to our Father in Heaven, no problem in*

*this world is too great for You. There is no drug or drink that can't be overcome by You, who bore my sins and died on the cross so I may be forgiven and set free. I ask for Your guidance and Your mighty right hand over my life Father. In Your precious son, Jesus Christs' name, Amen."*

Work to absorb the truth of that prayer and return to it as often as you need to call on Him.

3. "Then He said to her, 'Your sins are forgiven.' And those who sat at the table with Him began to say to themselves, 'Who is this who even forgives sins?' Then He said to the woman, 'Your faith has saved you. Go in peace.'" Luke 7:48-50

You will find me ruminating on page 213 saying, "The letter had been just what I needed. I was still holding the remaining pages, the 'Forgiveness Letter' he had enclosed." "So that's what he must have been talking about all that time. That thing to fill the voids is forgiveness," I tried processing it in my mind. "No way could 'forgiving' be the key to eliminate my voids, my drug addiction, the person I'd become," I questioned.

You've gotten to the point in your 30-day program where the "core theme" that was mentioned in the introduction, begins to reveal itself in Gary's letter to me. Gary had left me with two letters: the letter you just read in this chapter, and another letter that said "True Forgiveness" across the top. This is what led me to believe that "The Antidote for Addiction" the thing Gary had been pushing me to discover, was indeed forgiveness. However, I wasn't yet ready to read it, albeit because I wasn't yet able to "accept" it. We will dive further into this "True Forgiveness" letter and "The Antidote for Addiction" in the following days. But for now, let's answer some very basic questions surrounding forgiveness.

Are you carrying any type of burdens of resentment from unforgiveness?

If so, lay them out below. Get out as much as you can about them.

_____
_____
_____
_____
_____

Are you at a point in which you feel it's time to forgive those that seem to have caused the resentment? Explain why or why not.

_____
_____
_____
_____
_____

Let's rest with what you have just laid out. You have been pricked to respond in the manner you have and are beginning to grasp another perspective for issues such as these. You will be remembering this as you finish out the balance of Chapter 15 in Day 21 coming up. Re-read the chapter and I'll see you there.

# DAY 21

## CHAPTER 15

Alright my friend, you are about to embark on Day 21. When it is linked together with all the other days it will mean you have completed three weeks. Wow! Way to go. Everything you have done "In Christ" so far, is about to be supercharged. If you have re-read Chapter 15, you can begin your day with the empowering prayer:

*"Dear Lord, I enter this prayer in the name of Your son Jesus Christ. I pray and thank You for allowing my faith in You to come alive in me as I continue through this 30-day program. I know that it is by faith that I continue forward, as I'm seeking something that sometimes feels impossible to conquer. By trusting You, I know that anything is possible including faith in being delivered from drugs and alcohol. Your word says, "For by Grace you have been saved through faith." Father, I believe that by my faith in You, You will deliver me. In Jesus Christ's name, Amen."*

Now, let's explore the *Hand of God* in your circumstances.

## THE LOGAN EFFECT
## ...OR GODSCIDENCE

1. "And this is the will of Him who sent Me, that everyone who sees the Son and believes in Him may have everlasting life; and I will raise him up at the last day." John 6:40

On page 217 I lay out what my thoughts are when I say, "Logan's death was new to me and because I saw a little of myself in him, I felt like we'd known each other before. As he lay in a grave and I sat at my desk in my prison cell, questions began flooding over me. 'Why would you save me, a drug addict?' I thought. 'Why was I allowed to live and a promising young man like this and his teammates would be taken so young?' I continued asking these questions to God. I received no immediate response."

As a person attempting to step back "In Christ" after being lost for so many years, I had many questions that I felt God wasn't answering. "Why would you save me, a drug addict?" I asked God in my prison cell. Maybe you have also wondered why God allows such things. I've often asked myself, "Why do bad things happen to good people?" The answer, I discovered, is much simpler than I could have imagined. They don't! Bad things happen to good people, bad people, rich people, poor people, and any other type of person you can think of not just good people. As a Christian, the only concern our focus should be on while grieving over someone's death, is their position "In Christ." This would allow our prayer to be:

*"Dear God, my Hope and Trust is that they received and believed in your Son Jesus Christ while alive and they are with You now. That Your Peace and Comfort may come upon all their loved ones. In Jesus' Name I pray, Amen."*

Like Jesus said in the Scripture above, "everyone who sees the Son and believes in Him may have everlasting life." As Christians, some mistakenly believe death to be the worst thing that can happen to us. It is not, as death is simply a portal into the next step of everlasting life with God and His Son. A life in heaven filled with unimaginable peace, love, and joy.

Sometimes, it's hard to understand God's will, but it's not our job to always discern the human words for the magnitude of it. That task, often in difficult times like death, is much too great a feat for human comprehension, human intelligence. It is best to remember that He is God, and we are not. Yet, He does want us to recognize He is Sovereign over everything, and He has a purpose and a plan for everything. Then, it is resting in the Comfort that He offers to work through the days of pain in the physical loss.

Looking back now, I see how much God loved me. He gave me the opportunity to return to Him so that I too, could have a chance at everlasting life. Previously in your 30-day program, you were given an opportunity to surrender your life to Jesus Christ. It is my Hope and Trust that you have done this and are now a Child of the Living God Jesus Christ, having the Holy Spirit's Comfort and Counsel in your heart.

Please Note: You will find it difficult to move forward in the program if your new position "In Christ" has not been established.

Along with your forgiveness and salvation to God, through Christ, the need of the working of the Holy Spirit is paramount in discerning Spiritual things. Many Spiritual things are coming in the remaining days of your Deliverance Program. Paul explains it best when he wrote to the Church of Corinth, who like you needed to understand why this was important.

1Corinthians 2:12-14 says, "Now we (*Christians*) have received, not the spirit of the world, but the Spirit who is from God, that we might know the things that have been freely given to us by God. These things we also speak, not words that man's wisdom teaches but which the Holy Spirit teaches, comparing spiritual things with spiritual. But the natural man (*non-Christian*) does not receive the things of the Spirit of God, for they are foolishness to him; nor can he know them, because they are spiritually discerned." (*added*)

As you can see my hope for you is to be fully able to best discern what is to come and not have it be folly to you.

If you have not surrendered your life to Jesus Christ, I invite you to receive and believe in Him now. Please say this prayer with me:

*"Jesus, I trust you as my Lord and Savior. Please fill me with the Holy Spirit as I surrender my life to you, right now in the name of Jesus Christ. I acknowledge that You are King of my life, and I receive your free gift of salvation and everlasting life. In Jesus Christ's name, Amen."*

If you have surrendered your life to Jesus Christ, once again, welcome to the Kingdom. Pause for a moment and use this time in prayer to confess any sins you are harboring to God, through Jesus Christ. Embrace His Faithfulness and Justice in forgiving you and cleansing you. Feel free now to right down those things which you have been forgiven of in the Eyes of God.

_____
_____
_____
_____
_____
_____
_____

Nice work. Let God's Peace arise in you.

2. "Do you not know that those who run in a race all run, but one receives the prize? Run in such a way that you may obtain it." 1 Corinthians 9:24

On page 218 I begin to reveal my thoughts when I say, "What if my intentions grew into writing my story to help people like Logan had," I wondered. "To save lives as he did." I continued. "But my story is just another drug addict story, not like Logan's in the least." I pondered these ramblings as I closed the door to my footlocker. Then something Gary said in his farewell letter popped into my mind and caused me to think, "What new starting line had Gary been referring to?"

The "starting line" Gary was referring to is the starting line to the same race Paul is referring to in the Scripture above, a life surrendered to Jesus Christ and a life free from addictions. I sense that this race is rather more of a walk. It is our daily walk with Jesus Christ, In Jesus Christ, and through Jesus Christ. That walk, or relationship, is our daily living an "In Christ" Christian life. Gary knew that my new starting line lay ahead, my walk "In Christ" delivered from addiction. It wasn't pressured and it wasn't forced. Gary knew that because the Holy Spirit dwelt inside me, the same Holy Spirit would continue to assist me in growing closer to Him. He would help me run in such a way that I may receive the prize, winning the race in eternal life of the Kingdom, Heaven.

As someone who has surrendered their life to Jesus Christ, write below how are you running your race?

_____
_____
_____

Explain how close you feel your "In Christ" walk with Christ is.

_____
_____
_____

3. "So I say to you, ask, and it will be given to you; seek, and you will find; knock, and it will be opened to you. For everyone who asks receives, and he who seeks finds, and to him who knocks it will be opened." Luke 11:10-11

Continuing my pondering of these events on page 218 I say,

"As I was finishing up page 72 of the Sports Illustrated, I glanced over at the next page and sensed something I knew I would never forget, a coincidence of my life. A message. It was in that instant I heard, 'The ripples of the Logan Effect are still moving. Clearly, far out of Canada and right here into this Federal Prison Camp in North Carolina.' That very next page I had glanced at was an Ad Article for 'Partnership.' Their slogan is what pulled my eye, 'Hoping can't help a kid struggling with drugs. But together we can.' I laughed saying almost out loud 'Ain't that the truth!' The ad, sandwiched in between the pages of Logan's story said, 'We partner with parents and families to get help for kids whose drug or alcohol use threatens their lives with addiction.' Logan's story, my story! I was in awe. 'Out of all the ads in the magazine why this ad? Why this spot?' I asked myself. I continued thinking this as the last word I'd read reverberated through my head, 'Addiction.'"

As you see the title of this section is "Godscidence." Gary often used this term for "God orchestrated events," much greater than that of a mere "coincidence." These are those unexplainable events that seem to enter into your life by Divine intervention. Some faiths call it 'karma,' or some who struggle with the concept of God say it is perhaps the "universe" working. Yet, we as Christians call it for what it is, God! These are "Providentially and Perfectly Timed" events that you know without a shadow of a doubt could not have been lined up by the hand of man. These are "Godscidences." The truth is, that when you placed your faith in Jesus Christ, all things that you seek of God's will for your life, you will find, just as Jesus said above. Sometimes, these can even occur subconsciously. Subconsciously is the pricking of your spirit at the right time for the right thing. For me, I was finding a reason to finish my story, the book that you've been reading, "TATTOOS." I was knocking, and God had answered. What door was I knocking on? The door that would reveal the reason as to why I needed to finish my story. That door was the "Logan Effect" article being at the right place, at the right time, to be picked up by the right guy, me! How wonderful is it to know that anything we ask as Christians, God will make happen, according to His will for our lives. Pretty cool, right? The key is to be aware that God is always at work in and around you and to have your eyes, ears, and hands open to receive the Godscidences when He presents them in your life.

Take a few moments right now and explain a "Godscidence" in your life when He intervened, giving you an answer, or subconsciously a spiritual insight that you otherwise would not have discovered on your own.

_____

_____

_____

_____

Then, think of and write about the "Godscidence" that actually led you to be partaking in this 30-Day To Life Deliverance Program.

_____

_____

_____

_____

Pretty amazing once you open your eyes, ears, mind, and spirit to have it revealed. Something you thought was simply a coincidence turned out to truly be a Godscidence. Now, when that happens to you in the future, and you find yourself saying about a coincidence "Wow, that was amazing!" change it up immediately to "Wow, that was God!"

4. Continuing in the experience on page 220 I say,

"As I sat for a second in hopes of letting some of it settle, I recognized and decided to accept and say "This article was clearly meant for me to discover. Logan, his coach, my coach, the tattoos, the addiction ad, the Guardian Angels, all of it seemed to have come from a Higher Power." With that, another question came to me that I immediately directed toward God as I tried to process its implications. With Logan in mind, I asked, "What would he have wanted to tell his family before he died? What would he have wanted to tell himself? I'm sure he probably would have had a lot to say, had he known."

As I finished reading the article that day in my cell and thinking about Logan, I wondered what he may possibly have told himself before he died. Why was I asking this of Logan? I'm not quite sure, but I was beginning to feel like maybe God was working inside me, tugging at me to figure something out. So, I continued with my eyes, ears, hands, mind, and spirit open.

At this point in your 30-day program, I want you to put yourself in that position of reflection. You may lean on my Logan story Godscidence for now or go directly to a personal one that you had or are currently experiencing.

Write out the Godscidence you are reflecting on.

_____
_____
_____
_____

Now, answer these questions.

What are you telling yourself about it right now as you're talking to yourself, giving yourself advice?

_____
_____
_____
_____

Here is an opportunity to put on paper what the talk is in your head. It can be anything. No right or wrong for now, just experiencing it.

5. The revelation came on page 223 where I say,

"In that moment I knew what I had to do. Stepping off the track I headed back towards my cell. I had something to read I'd been ignoring. Something that wouldn't start with my family or friends. It would start with myself. I got to my cell and flung my footlocker open grabbing the 'Forgiveness Letter.' I was now searching for a way to forgive myself with an overwhelming feeling that it was something this entire road had been leading to. I hopped into my bed, cracked open the letter the Old Man had left me, and read...."

At the end of "The Logan Effect" chapter, everything begins to fall into place. Between "The Logan Effect" article and my conversation with Mike on the track, you are witnessing me beginning to realize that maybe I need to forgive myself. First though, I knew I needed to read Gary's 'Forgiveness Letter.'

As these "Godscidences" came into my life, and I thought about forgiveness of self, I remember trying to tell myself that there couldn't possibly be "anything" I needed to forgive myself for. (A case of me giving myself advise yet being tugged by the Holy Spirit's guidance that there was more.)

Previously in the book, when I was sentenced by the judge, I read a letter "asking" for forgiveness from my family and friends, but I hadn't thought about forgiving myself until now, upon reading the 'Forgiveness Letter.'

At this point in your 30-day program, I believe you are ready to think about some things that you'd like to forgive yourself for. Make a list of as many as you can. Ready...Go!

1. _____
2. _____
3. _____
4. _____
5. _____

Well done my friend. Rest for now with the list. You will be guided shortly as to what to do with it. For now, you accomplished a lot. Thank the Lord for your great day. When you are ready read Chapter 16, and I will see you at day 22.

# DAY 22

## CHAPTER 16

Welcome to Day 22. Having re-read Chapter 16 you sense it is time to bring forgiveness home for you and let it play out in your life. Begin with your daily prayer:

*"Dear Lord, I enter this prayer in the name of Your son Jesus Christ. I pray and thank You for allowing my faith in You to come alive in me as I continue through this 30-day program. I know that it is by faith that I continue forward, as I'm seeking something that sometimes feels impossible to conquer. By trusting You, I know that anything is possible including faith in being delivered from drugs and alcohol. Your word says, "For by Grace you have been saved through faith." Father, I believe that by my faith in You, You will deliver me. In Jesus Christ's name, Amen."*

Now that you have been reminded that the Good Lord is on board, you are ready to engage.

## PERSONALIZED FORGIVENESS...
## ...'TO' ME

1. "Repent therefore of this your wickedness, and pray God if perhaps the thought of your heart may be forgiven you. For I see that you are poisoned by bitterness and bound by iniquity." Acts 8:22-23

Gary finds himself dealing with the tenets of this very scripture in his letter to me on pages 225 and 226 as he says,

"One day out of pure frustration, I asked myself, 'Why am I not forgiving this person? I know it says somewhere that I am supposed to. I know it says somewhere that it is the best thing for me to do. But I don't. Why don't I? Why not now? Why not before now?' Then I heard this inside my head... You're not really digging very hard to find out the 'why.' You're somehow comfortable in the misery of being mad and angry. You continue to be bound by the negative thoughts of it all! You're just not ready! You still see forgiving as surrendering. You still see forgiving as just not fair! Just not deserving of him! Just not right! You are just not comfortable with him getting 'no condemnation' for what he has done to you. You suffered so why shouldn't he?"

A lot of us, and I mean a LOT of us, associate forgiveness with the thought of negative submission. If you're like me in the least, submission is a hard pill to swallow, especially if we feel as if we're submitting to someone that we feel has wronged us. Before we know it, we're "somehow comfortable in the misery of being mad and angry. You continue to be bound by the negative thoughts of it all," like Gary says in the letter. Finally, most of us choose not to forgive, because we feel as if we're giving the individual that's wronged us, "the easy way out." We feel as if some sort of "revenge" is warranted. All of these lies, circulating around forgiveness, are planted by Satan in hopes of sowing seeds of resentment, that when full grown, lead to massive damage internally that often becomes one of the root causes of our addictions. When you need to kill a weed in your garden, you don't just pull off the top of the dandelion, it will almost always come back. To be healed of our addictions, we need to attack the root, the cause. Resentment of some sort is commonly the root cause of our addictions. Fix the resentment and you'll more than likely begin to fix your addictions. Forgiveness is the only way. Yet, the devil doesn't want us to know this, why? Because he wants us to remain sinning and miserable.

Throughout your 30-day program, I've challenged you to think about different people you feel you may hold resentment towards. Now, let's get specific. Think about one person that you feel you hold the greatest deal of resentment towards. Write their name below.

_____

Don't think of, or dwell on the pain that person's name tries to bring up, just rest with writing it down for now.

2. "But that you may know that the Son of Man has power on earth to forgive sins…" Mark 2:10

Gary continues in his letter to speak of the assurance of change on page 226 and 227 where he says,

"In a positively dramatic way, it will. That's because it is about God's plan and God's picture for your life, not yours. There is a Higher calling and a Higher purpose for you to be going through all this. A purpose that has nothing to do with your control or reasoning, but God's alone. You have been unwilling to yield to this, therefore, you not only don't forgive, but you also can't forgive! No one truly and completely forgives outside of God. It is a Spiritual phenomenon, not a human one."

Now that you understand who you need to apply forgiveness to (the person you identified above), you now need to understand who it is that's going to help you rid your mind of the burdens of resentment. You see, "Intellectual Forgiveness" is forgiveness on a human level. This forgiveness will never work long range, let alone short range, why? Because God is the only One that can truly, once and for all time, forgive sins, not man. "No one truly and completely forgives outside of God. It is a Spiritual phenomenon," as Gary says. Understand that this is the key component of our deliverance from drugs and alcohol addiction. How many times have you tried to forgive, only to have those feelings of bitterness come right back to the surface at the next stumbling of the offender? You see what I mean? Forgiveness applied by humans doesn't work effectively, yet forgiveness with God does. Forgiving someone through God's forgiveness is called "Spiritually Graced Forgiveness." This became possible since the death and resurrection of Jesus Christ. This is why it's so important to place your faith in Jesus Christ with the hope of being delivered into sobriety from any kind of addiction.

Because of faith, you were saved through Grace, God's Grace! Grace here means "unmerited favor" because He first loves you and not because you have earned it by your work. His Son's death on the cross, allows you a unique advantage to be able to forgive others truly and completely, thus killing the primary root cause of your addictions, resentment toward another's transgressions against you. What I'm writing, Satan does not want you to know. As a matter of fact, do you know how many times these revelations almost didn't make it to paper and print? Satan threw an innumerable number of obstacles in the way of Gary and me, our families, and friends, and even here in prison, in an attempt to never allow this truth to come to light in TATTOOS, let alone your 30 Daysto Life Deliverance Program. So, please don't take this information you just read lightly. You've just been allowed to discover "The Antidote for Addiction" and the cure to your debilitating addiction, "Spiritually Graced Forgiveness," the Deliverance!

Finish today by taking some time to meditate and pray over the things revealed by Gary on page 227 referencing Jesus' actions. Go there and see if you can see why Gary says,

*'No one truly and completely forgives outside of God, as even Jesus went to God. "Father, forgive them, for they know not what they do." (Lk 23:34)*

*'It is by God that you forgive, not by you alone.*

*It is you asking God to forgive them.*

*It is you asking God to forgive you, first.*

*It is you asking God to remove the pain of these transgressions.*

*He forgives them.*

*He forgives you.*

*He gives you Peace, beyond all understanding.*

*He frees you up to move on with your life, bigger and better for it.'*

I remain proud of you for continuing to engage the exercises and questions. I trust that the Holy Spirit in you is allowing you to see what you are experiencing and what lay ahead for you "In Christ."

Be sure to re-read the balance of Chapter 16 and I will look forward to seeing you at Day 23.

# DAY 23

## CHAPTER 16

Well, it looks like you are ready to jump into Day 23 and continue the next part of Chapter 16. Begin again with your now habitual daily program prayer:

*"Dear Lord, I enter this prayer in the name of Your son Jesus Christ. I pray and thank You for allowing my faith in You to come alive in me as I continue through this 30-day program. I know that it is by faith that I continue forward, as I'm seeking something that sometimes feels impossible to conquer. By trusting You, I know that anything is possible including faith in being delivered from drugs and alcohol. Your word says, "For by Grace you have been saved through faith." Father, I believe that by my faith in You, You will deliver me. In Jesus Christ's name, Amen."*

Remember, with the Good Lord on Board, you go.

## PERSONALIZED FORGIVENESS...
## ...'TO' ME (CONT.)

1. Before I call on you to begin writing your own forgiveness letter to the person you wrote down in the previous day, let's take a look at the steps highlighted on page 232. These are as Gary best heard

them when he asked God to reveal the next best course of action. The hope is for you to gain a better understanding of "Spiritually Graced Forgiveness." Ask the Good Lord to Guide your thoughts and understanding of the steps. Take as much time as you need to review them so that you are moved to really know what is before you:

1. Ask God to forgive you personally for all you have harbored toward this person and in the situation.

2. Ask God to forgive them for *all* they have harbored toward you and in the situation.

3. Write out a note of forgiveness stating that you have been forgiven by God and now you are forgiving them completely and will be praying for their peace going forward.

4. Now, forgive them by reading the note out loud allowing your emotions to be released and restored.

5. Say a prayer of Healing, Goodness, and Peace into their life. (A blessing like in 1 Peter 3:4)

6. Thank God for the gift of this forgiveness.

7. Receive your *forgiveness*\* as it is now complete.

\*This forgiveness is not predicated on you sending them the note, reading it to them, and/or them accepting it! This is about your freedom from unforgiveness.

Go to the top of page 233 and finish reading the complete (\*) paragraph to get a better grasp on how Gary feels this is playing out for you from God's perspective.

Now, review the prayer (from page 228 in TATTOOS) and note of Gary's to see how he responded to God's "Call to Action."

Gary's prayer to God:

*"Dear God please forgive me for my unforgiveness. Please forgive him also. Help me to begin the process of forgiving him. Please help me to find peace within this life and for him also. Give me the strength to know that you have a plan not only for me in all of this but for him. Help me to remember that I, as well as he, can only be convicted to change through you, in your way, in your season, for your reason. And that I am only capable and responsible for how and when I respond to this process of change in me and not him. He is in your hands, not mine. I am now in your hands. Thank you."*

'Note of Forgiveness' to his father

'Dad, I want you to know that as much as I have hated you over these years, in some way I have loved you more. I am sick and tired of harboring these awful, negative feelings toward you. I am tired of trying to figure out an answer to why you would possibly have treated me the way you did. Why you would have been so seemingly mean in your actions and your words toward me over the years. I had hoped that you would sense the pain that you had caused me and out of love for me come forward and accepted it, apologized for it, and helped me heal from it. This had never happened which in itself seemed to continually add to my pain. But something amazing has happened to me today that I want to share with you and then give you something. Today, as I once again was muddling over my pain and woes seemingly at your hands, God came to me in my thoughts and forgave me. Yes, he forgave me for all the awful, hurtful, vindictive, and vengeful thoughts I have had toward you over this. He actually forgave me when I thought if anyone needed this forgiveness it was you, not me! But I realized then and there that He was right. That no matter what you had done and why you had done it to me it was wrong for me to react in such a way. So, he forgave me, even though I had done nothing to be worthy of such forgiveness. As soon as that happened something incredible came over me. I no longer wanted to be mad at you. I no longer wanted to be 'pissed off' at you. I no longer wanted to be frustrated with you. I was tired of it. And just like that its appeal was gone. Yes, really gone. Therefore, I want you to know that from this moment forward I forgive you, period, I hold nothing against you for any of your past words or actions toward me. And I pray that you may find peace within all of this yourself. This is now between you and God and no longer me. You are free from my wrath. I harbor it no more. I give it to you freely, as it was given to me. I love you. Gary'

Can you see and feel how the release came about and by *who's* hand?

Breathe that all in for a moment, then continue.

2. Application of "Spiritually Graced Forgiveness" which you now know is "The Antidote for Addiction"!

Now, after better understanding the steps to "Spiritually Graced Forgiveness" and reviewing both Gary's prayer and letter to his father, I'd like you to apply the same steps.

**Step #1** by praying to God asking God to forgive you for all you have harbored against this person.

**Step #2**, Ask God to forgive them for all they have harbored towards you.

**Step #3**, write out your note of forgiveness to the person you just prayed over. Pause right here and let the Holy Spirit in you be your guide to write.

_____
_____
_____
_____

Good job my friend. Take a short breather and find a quiet, private place.

**Step #4.** Read the note aloud.

Well done!

Now, bring it all home by completing steps 5, 6, & 7!

**Step #5**: Say a prayer, of Healing, Goodness, and Peace into their life. (A blessing like in 1 Peter 3:4 from the "…hidden person of the heart, with the incorruptible beauty of a gentle and quiet spirit, which is very precious in the sight of God.") Write the prayer out here.

_____
_____
_____
_____

You will soon be asked to continue a daily blessing prayer for them and may choose to use this one.

**Step #6**: Thank God for this forgiveness and healing. Write down how you thanked Him.

_____
_____
_____
_____

This will become a pattern of the great times ahead when you thank Him anew at His many blessings.

**Step #7**: Receive your 'forgiveness' as it is now complete (page 232 0f TATTOOS). Write out what that feels like to you, including any emotion that has touched you through your following through on your Spiritually Graced Forgiveness.

_____
_____
_____
_____

Amazing! And what do we call this type of amazing?... God!

Allow the feeling of peace and joy to enter your life, as Jesus Christ has taken the burden of resentment from you and shown you first-hand how to deal with it moving forward as you live Delivered.

What a day. So glad you completed it. Even with all that, there is more excitement ahead. Why wouldn't there be, it is your new life "In Christ" right?

Be sure to read the ... 'From Me' section of Chapter 16 and I will see you at Day 24!

# DAY 24

## CHAPTER 16

Welcome back. Day 24 brings you to the third part of Chapter 16. Let's continue your journey with your opening prayer:

*"Dear Lord, I enter this prayer in the name of Your son Jesus Christ. I pray and thank You for allowing my faith in You to come alive in me as I continue through this 30-day program. I know that it is by faith that I continue forward, as I'm seeking something that sometimes feels impossible to conquer. By trusting You, I know that anything is possible including faith in being delivered from drugs and alcohol. Your word says, "For by Grace you have been saved through faith." Father, I believe that by my faith in You, You will deliver me. In Jesus Christ's name, Amen."*

Now, you have been reminded that the Good Lord is on board. It would be best to remember your reading and working with the "Forgiveness Letter" of Day 23 "To Me" as you jump in.

## PERSONALIZED FORGIVENESS...
## ...'FROM' ME.

1. On page 233 I open up more of my world to you when I say, "I put the letter down and stared forward at the white brick in my

cell. A room free from stimuli. The institution I occupied was a colorless cage. Drab at best. My vision usually searching for some resemblance of color in here. Now, however, my eyes fixed forward in a trance. Unblinking, I couldn't see past what I'd just read. 'The Forgiveness Letter,' a blueprint to uncovering a life of peace. Or so he said. Yet, I doubted its effectiveness for me. 'Could it work? I whispered. He had waited to give me this until he left. I was pissed. I had questions. A solution all this time, crumpled in my footlocker. I was seething to get to the new starting line.' 'You knew this is what I needed though, didn't you?' A question I asked the old man that wasn't there. He knew that this too was part of the story. The journey of discovery."

After reading "The Forgiveness Letter" Gary left for me, the same letter that contained the steps you just utilized in your previous day's work, I doubted its effectiveness. Maybe you can relate. Really though, I was doubting God's effectiveness, because that's Who is helping me to forgive in the first place. The only One capable of forgiving.

I didn't apply "The Antidote for Addiction" with other people in my life until after I had written the one to myself first, as you'll soon be re-reading or rediscovering in the book. At this point in my journey, I knew that to begin moving forward, I needed to begin by forgiving myself. Through my drug addiction, I had created quite the havoc on many people's lives. I blamed myself for much. It's only by the Grace of God, and the pricking of the Holy Spirit in me that I came to realize that if it was to stop, it would have to start with me. I'm certain that you yourself have either come to this gripping realization or are working your very best to. I know this because the Holy

Spirit has been tugging at you, like He did me, and empowering you for your commitment to persevere. I know this because you've made it all the way to Day 24 in this program! Congratulations!

Yet, the journey continues. Pause right now and write a list of all the things you feel you still hold "against yourself." The goal here is begin brainstorming, like I did, before writing a forgiveness letter to yourself. Ask the Good Lord to free your mind to be able to see all that you harbor and then begin.

_____
_____
_____
_____
_____
_____
_____
_____
_____
_____

Good Job. You have now armed yourself with the very things God is about to deal with.

2. You can see the battle of my mind over the vision of my previous self on page 234 where I say,

"The 'Dear Cody' had forced him out, eradicated his hold from the host that was me. Now, I could see him in his ugliness, the nasty addicted human he was. I stared at the Cody staring back at me, was afraid of what I saw. A monster. Fearful and unkind he had been born out of unforgiveness. Of course, the letter was proving that. I put the pen back to the paper and began to write again."

Maybe you're like me. Maybe you feel that there is something inside you, some darkness, that you'd like to eradicate. This was the "Perfect Storm" that created the "voids" within me. These are the very "voids" that I tried so hard to quell with drugs, sex, and alcohol. You've applied the "Antidote for Addiction" forgiveness on someone else in your life the previous day, but now it's time to apply it to yourself. It's time to do what I was so fearful of doing myself, forgiving myself and giving these burdens to the only One that can bear them, Jesus Christ.

Pause and begin by writing only "Dear (your name)" on the top of this work section, then before you begin writing the rest of your letter to yourself stop and pray:

*"Jesus Christ, I come to Your throne boldly asking for You to guide me as I release all of the burdens that I've been carrying in regard to all the times I've wronged myself before you over the years. Lord God, as I continue forward in writing this letter to myself, I repent of any and all sins that are written, spoken, or thought during this process. Jesus, I know You and You alone have the ability to give me a clean slate and a clean bill of health, ridding my body of this storm Father, this addiction. May your forgiveness lift this burden from me Father, for You have already bourn these burdens on the cross. I pray these things in the name of Jesus Christ, Amen"*

Now begin where you left off and let the Holy Spirit guide your pace, your revelation of self, and your words in reply to what you see.

Ok, begin writing your forgiveness letter to yourself.

Dear_____,
        (your name)

_____
_____
_____
_____
_____
_____
_____
_____
_____
_____
_____
_____
_____
_____
_____

Way to go! No matter if you feel it is in rough form, you allowed yourself to begin to put words to your life and yourself.

You are now ready to dive into putting the final touches on your letter and how to activate it for your new "In Christ" self. When you are ready, have your TATTOOS book open to page 235 and turn to Day 25. See you there.

# DAY 25

## CHAPTER 16

Welcome back my friend. What a leap you made in Day 24. You will be continuing in that theme and position today in preparation for your Journey into 'The New Antidote.' Begin again with your prayer:

*"Dear Lord, I enter this prayer in the name of Your son Jesus Christ. I pray and thank You for allowing my faith in You to come alive in me as I continue through this 30-day program. I know that it is by faith that I continue forward, as I'm seeking something that sometimes feels impossible to conquer. By trusting You, I know that anything is possible including faith in being delivered from drugs and alcohol. Your word says, "For by Grace you have been saved through faith." Father, I believe that by my faith in You, You will deliver me. In Jesus Christ's name, Amen."*

Once again, you have been reminded that the Good Lord is on Board. Let's continue.

## PERSONALIZED FORGIVENESS ...'FROM' ME. (CONT.)

1. "God, I am sorry for the person I was and can still be at times." (excerpt from Cody's note to himself on page 235

Now in full, read out to page 237,

"Dear Cody, I'm sorry for putting you in this place, you shouldn't be here.

You're an amazing person with a ton of potential Cody. I know this place isn't where you want to be, but you know it's what you needed. To forgive yourself. To face yourself, clean and drug-free. You were caught in a terrible addiction and I'm so glad you're alive. We have an amazing life ahead of us. God, I am sorry for the person I was and can still be at times. All I care about is this point forward, not the past. The New Starting Line.

I don't care about your voids anymore Cody. They are in the past. From this point forward you will be void-free. You will fill your voids with the love from God, not drugs or alcohol. Cody, you're important to a lot of people. Your family and friends, they love you immensely. When you get done with this letter, you're going to write a forgiveness letter to all of them. You're going to forgive them, and they are going to forgive you. This will happen because God will forgive you. You are the rose that is just as beautiful as a seed as you are a flower. You're a ten Cody, in God's eyes, you've always been a ten. You're not an addict or a loser, weak or unworthy. Cody, you're the opposite of those things. You're strong and vibrant. Life radiates from you, and you don't need drugs or alcohol to validate that. YOU see that. The only person you need to follow is God, his validation is the only validation you need. Cody, I forgive you forever. Stop thinking otherwise. Stop chasing this validation from others. You're free of that and I forgive you. Cody, you're going to go through some things in life that aren't your fault, so don't blame yourself. Love yourself and know that God will always love you back. Say your prayers before bed and always smile kid. You're perfect the way you are, don't change for anyone. I love you, buddy."

You have just re-read the note I wrote to myself and God. Notice I didn't exactly follow Gary's blueprint, and that's ok, as Gary's steps are predicated on forgiving someone else. I have rewritten them for the steps in forgiving yourself, combining steps 1 and 2.

1. Ask God to forgive you for all you have harbored towards yourself.

2. Write out a "note of forgiveness" stating that you have been forgiven by God, you are accepting that forgiveness completely, forgiving yourself, and will be praying for your peace going forward.

3. Now, forgive yourself by reading the note out loud allowing your emotions and pain to be released and peace restored.

4. Say a Prayer of Healing, Goodness, and Peace into your life.

5. Thank God for the gift of this forgiveness.

6. Receive your `forgiveness' as it is now complete.

Ok, this is your time, this is your season. You now have a model in my note and the revised blueprint in steps, so begin with your prayer asking God to forgive you. Ready? Set? Forgive!

Writing this personal 'note of forgiveness' to yourself may be emotionally challenging for you, as it was for me, but let God guide you to freely say what needs to be said to yourself. He is with you.

Dear _____,
　　　　　(your name)

_____
_____
_____
_____
_____
_____
_____
_____
_____
_____
_____
_____
_____
_____
_____
_____

I am so, so proud of you. This is a big weight that has been released from your shoulders. Rest comfortably tonight. This is what it feels like as the new you, "In Christ."

When you are ready read Chapter 17 and get prepared for Day 26. See you there.

# DAY 26

## CHAPTER 17

You continue to amaze me! Your "note of forgiveness" to yourself is complete and you are ready to go full on into Day 26 to continue bringing your journey alive. I trust you have re-read Chapter 17, so head on into your daily prayer:

**\*\*\* Embrace the language in your NEW PROGRAM PRAYER:**

"Dear Lord, I enter this prayer in the name of Your son Jesus Christ. I pray and thank You for allowing my faith in You to come alive in me as I continue through this 30-day program. I know that it is by faith that I continue forward, as I'm seeking something that sometimes feels impossible to conquer. By trusting You, I know that anything is possible including faith in being delivered from drugs and alcohol. Your word says, "For by Grace you have been saved through faith." Father, I believe that by my faith in You, I am Delivered. In Jesus Christ's name, Amen."

Your momentum is in full force and will be carrying you into...

## THE NEW ANDTIDOTE...
## ...RECOGNITION

1. "Therefore, if anyone is in Christ, he is a new creation; old things have passed away; behold, all things have become new." 2 Corinthians 5:17

I share my ponderings of the man on the track on page 241 saying,

"I couldn't believe how much of myself I saw in him so instantly. Maybe it was the stature. Maybe it was the other features. His haircut perhaps. Or maybe it was what he transmitted that I felt. Energy from him to me. A pain? A sadness? A void?"

Now that you've experienced deliverance through God's healing power, you'll begin to notice small changes in your life, "old things have passed away, behold, all things have become new," as the Scripture above says. There are many great new things about being "In Christ" living delivered and being free from the burdens of resentment. One change is that things from your former life seem to no longer interest you. It may take some time and a few defining incidents for your mind to really recognize this spiritual change. Don't fight it, embrace it. When old obsessions do not appear, don't call them in. Enjoy the fact that they do not attach themselves naturally to you anymore. Simply pause and say, "Thank You God!"

Also, being delivered from your addictions means that you are now able to begin, in some small way to help those who are struggling with addictions themselves. Please understand that for them to witness you "living Delivered" is your first and best way to be a present help to them.

I am going to ask you to pause for a few moments to read and reread the following Scripture until you see yourself in it. Then, I encourage you to use it to stand on its Truth when strength is needed in your "living Delivered" life.

"He has delivered us (*me*) from the power of darkness and has conveyed us (*me*) into the kingdom of the Son of His love, in whom we (*I*) have redemption through His blood, the forgiveness of sins."

Colossians 1:13,14 (*added*)

In Chapter 17 you were able to meet Tanner, a young man I met here in prison. I was able to see some of myself in him, and like the passage from the book reads, I could sense his voids. Now that you've been delivered, you can better recognize more than just the "face" of addiction. With that understanding and experience, you may be pricked in the spirit for someone you know that could benefit from it. Someone who the Good Lord is calling you to share the healing power of Jesus Christ in their life of suffering in addiction. Pray on it. Move when He calls you to move. Remember, being present is the first thing. Then, though engaging may seem strange at first, as you yourself are just recently adjusting to living a life free from your addictions, the Holy Spirit will guide you. Rest in His patience with them. Use the voice and tools that He makes available to you. **It will be Him that moves their spirit, not you.**

At this point in your 30-day program, take a moment and think about some of the people close to you in your life that may be suffering, or you know for sure are suffering from an addiction of their own. Below, write 5 names of people that you can pray about for God's direction in reaching out to share your story and introduce them to 'The Antidote for Addiction', Spiritually Graced Forgiveness!

1._____
2._____
3._____
4._____
5._____

Now, say this prayer, listen for His voice, and be obedient to what direction He points you in:

*"Dear God, Thank you for Your deliverance of me from my addiction. I pray for (names) who as you know, are continuing to struggle with addiction. May You guide me as to when and how You are calling me to reach out to them. When you ask me to act, please give me Your timing and words to share with them. I pray all of this in Jesus Christ's Name, Amen."*

Relax and know that you will know when He speaks. If He already has, then move on His word. If He hasn't be sure to show up where He speaks and be open to His Voice.

## ...INJECTION

2. "Therefore, as the elect of God, holy and beloved, put on tender mercies, kindness, humility, meekness, longsuffering; bearing with one another, and forgiving one another, if anyone has a complaint against another; even as Christ forgave you, so you also must do." Colossians 3:12-13

On page 245 you will feel my state of mind when I say, "I had no idea what to do. I recognized that I wasn't equipped for this kind of conversation, or so the negative voice told me. "This kind of healing isn't for you," the voice said. I sat back down and started praying, "God, please help me say the right things to this kid. You helped me write this story and discover myself, now please help me to help others do the same."

Tanner wasn't in reality one individual, but a culmination into a fictitious character. Tanner represents the combined interactions I've had with numerous inmates regarding addiction. Though Tanner is many people in one, I assure you, the conversation I had with Tanner happened many times with many men. In fact, at first, I was nervous in speaking to other men. Yes, the feelings of unworthiness crept back into my psyche, "This kind of healing isn't for you," the unholy, unhealthy voice of Satan attempting to convince me. I'm quite certain you probably feel the

same way in just reading, praying, hearing, and being instructed to reach out. Maybe one of the names you wrote down is a longtime friend you've used drugs with. Maybe one of the people you wrote down is a family member. Perhaps they are the very person that introduced you to drugs and/or alcohol. Maybe, if you are in the program in prison, it's an inmate you hang out with every day and you consider them a brother or friend. Whoever they are, it doesn't matter if you have been called to reach out. What does matter is that you've received the gift of deliverance from your addictions, and who are we to hide that amazing knowledge when called upon? As an old saying goes, "It is not that I am qualified, it is that I am equipped, only because I have been 'Called'."

Despite what voice Satan may use in trying to convince you that "you are not qualified," it's important to press on. You must spread the word of "Spiritually Graced Forgiveness" wherever and whenever you are called to do so. When you do, you will tell others that "It is possible to be delivered from your addiction by the healing of your burdens of resentment through Jesus Christ."

Could you imagine for a moment if we reached the point in this world where EVERYONE, EVERYWHERE FORGAVE, ALL THE TIME?

Let's say a prayer as we move forward:

*"Jesus Christ please give me the courage and wisdom as I continue forward. Jesus, I thank You for delivering me from the burdens of unforgiveness and for delivering me from my addictions. Please help me to hear Your Voice as to where and when you want me to spread this amazing news to people suffering from addiction. It's no longer about just me Father, it's about other people I love and care about that are still in bondage to the things I was in bondage to. Thank you. In the name of Jesus Christ, Amen."*

## ...INJECTION/...LIBERATION

3. "Jesus said to him, "I am the way, the truth, and the life. No one comes to the Father except through Me." John 14:6

On page 248 near the end of my interaction you can hear my excitement when I say,

"Can you believe it's as easy as recognizing your importance and letting all your burdens go by writing forgiveness letters to yourself and all those you hold animosity towards?" he said through short-filled gasps. I said the only thing I could really think to say at that moment, "God is wonderful isn't he Tanner, as in doing it for us He showed us the way?"

Clearly, you can see the importance of recognizing that all glory goes to Jesus Christ who sacrificed Himself to make this possible for us. I don't want people to associate my name or Gary's name in any way with what makes "The Antidote for Addiction" possible. I want everyone to see Jesus Christ and what He did on the cross and what He does daily for each of us to make this possible. There is "Spiritually Graced Forgiveness" Power in the blood of Jesus Christ. There is the presence of the Holy Spirit that dwells inside us by our receiving and believing in Him. If one places their faith in Jesus Christ as Lord and Savior, the same power that raised Jesus from the dead, is the same power that heals and delivers that person from their painful addiction. At God's Calling it becomes the responsibility of every believer to spread this message, even more so to those suffering from an addiction. The message begins with the light of Christ that shines from you as you live your delivered life.

At this point in your 30-day program, I'd like you to pick one of the people you wrote down in Exercise 1 and pray to God specifically for them. Then apply these steps.

1. Let them know, in whatever way God calls you to, that they are worthy in His eyes through His Son Jesus Christ. Remember 'The Story of the Rose' Chapter 13. Use it as a reference, where need be.

2. Tell them 'Your Journey' story, include your discovery of "The Antidote for Addiction" in the TATTOOS book and how "Spiritually Graced Forgiveness" delivered you from your addictions.

3. Tell them how the Good Lord called you to reach out to them.

4. Show them the TATOOS book and The 30 Days to Life Deliverance Program, introducing them to www.antidoteforaddiction.com and encourage them to engage personally, beginning with the book.

5. Pray with them. Trust the Holy Spirit in you to have the words for them.

6. Write out your experience with this assignment.

_____
_____
_____
_____
_____
_____
_____
_____
_____
_____
_____

I pray for you the very best as you continue forward on this wonderful journey, Your Delivered Life Journey. God's got you!

"Now may the God of hope fill you with all joy and peace in believing, that you may abound in hope by the power of the Holy Spirit."

Romans 15:13

Read the Epilogue and I will see you at Day 27.

# DAY 27

## EPILOGUE

Welcome, welcome to the Epilogue. Begin today with your updated prayer of affirmation:

*"Dear Lord, I enter this prayer in the name of Your son Jesus Christ. I pray and thank You for allowing my faith in You to come alive in me as I continue through this 30-day program. I know that it is by faith that I continue forward, as I'm seeking something that sometimes feels impossible to conquer. By trusting You, I know that anything is possible including faith in being delivered from drugs and alcohol. Your word says, "For by Grace you have been saved through faith." Father, I believe that by my faith in You, I am Delivered. In Jesus Christ's name, Amen."*

Fantastic. Knowing the Good Lord is on Board, begin.

## A LASTING NARCAN

1. I open from my position of deliverance on page 248 and 249 saying,

"Although the negative voices still exist, I believe them to have no real power over my life anymore. It was incredibly liberating to discover my true worth, because the darkness that had aimed to consume me, was crippling me. By finally understanding and accepting my importance first to God and then to myself, I've been able to fill my painful voids with love. So, it doesn't really matter what the negative voices try to convince me of now, they're called out as gibberish and relegated back to the low place from which they came."

The fact is, when you work to grow your relationship with God, the devil will attempt to trip you up and prevent that closeness. He is the same voice that caused you to falter into addiction. Recognizing his tactics and how he is able to do that, means that you can be better prepared for them. Being aware is the first step in being equipped. Never forget this. But how do you overcome his voice, his tactics, and get better and better at dealing with them and him? As a soldier in Christ, your offensive and defensive strategies against the darkness are the same: Jesus Christ. You will remember that throughout this program I have led you to call on His name in everything, from prayer to actions. You cannot and will not defeat the enemy on your own. However, you can and will defeat him by leaning more and more into Jesus Christ.

As a believer Mark 16:17 says "…in My name you will cast out demons, …" Therefore, **you now have His permission to use the name of Jesus, to cast out Satan in the Name of Jesus Christ.**

Jesus gives you an example of speaking directly to Satan, the devil, demon, minion, fiend, imp, and his deceptive lying voice in Matthew 16:21-23 when He says, "Get behind Me, Satan! You are an offense to Me, for you are not mindful of the things of God, but the things of men."

Now, You "In Christ" through the power of Jesus' mighty name, have the ability to send Satan and his lying voice packing when there is any challenge to tempt and torment you. You have heard me utilize Him in this way within this program. Here is an example of what it may sound like for you when you find yourself with the voice of the enemy nipping at thoughts in your head or tugging at you through someone else's voice of temptation:

"Satan, in the Name of Jesus Christ I cast you and your lying voice out of my head and my thoughts, into the abyss. Leave me at once as your voice has no power or hold over me in the name of Jesus Christ."

You will need to practice, practice, and practice this until it becomes a natural habit. I encourage you to follow-up that casting out command with a call to the Good Lord like this:

"Dear God, fill the space of my thoughts and mind created by the casting out of Satan and his voice, with your Holy Spirit voice of *truth*. May I continue to walk upright in You. In Jesus' name I pray, Amen."

That is the way to cast Satan out when you find him in your midst.

Now to keep him at bay, so to speak, your best defense is working to not idly find yourself in his midst. The way to do just that is **stay grounded daily in God's Word, yes, the Scriptures**. To come up with an excuse as to not being able to find the time, is to accept Satan's lying voice. If you hear that foolishness, cast it out immediately.

Here is how it works: You don't find time to get into the Word, you make time. You prioritize time. You make it as if it is the breath that you spiritually breathe to stay alive in Deliverance.

**Couple this with prayer**. This is conversational praise, petition, and thanksgiving prayer time set aside every day, and spontaneously throughout the day. When I shared with you the scripture speaking to 'pray without ceasing' let me help you with what that means. It means knowing and keeping open the Holy Spirit's voice from the moment you come awake to the time you go to sleep. Go to him throughout your day in anything and everything. Keep Him involved in all you do. You do not have to set an appointment as He is always right there waiting for the conversation. Sometimes it will be Him pricking you or tugging at you to reach out. Other times you will find yourself in the middle of trying to get out of a quagmire in your work, business, or life and realize you are going it alone, and you then reach out. This is what I call having everything you do be Holy Spirit Driven and Prayerfully Achieved. Begin today, right now doing just that. Over time in practicing, practicing, and practicing you will come to own it!

Now, wrap all this with the living, breathing spiritual glue that holds it all together and wreaks havoc with Satan's desire to have his voice heard. **That is Christian Fellowship**. Having, keeping, developing, and growing in a fellowship with other Christians where you can lay out and share each other's joys in Christ and burdens in life. Learning how to apply the tenets of your Christian walk alongside of others. Pray about it, and the Holy Spirit will prick your heart as to where that is to happen for you. Do not miss this one.

Finally, **guard your eyes, ears, hands, and mouth from the trappings of the secular world.** Listen to Christian Radio, read Christian books, both Non-fiction and Fiction. Reach your Christian hand out to others. Speak with the voice from the Holy Spirit in you. Scripture says no man can bridle his tongue. That being true means to bridle it, you will need more than you. You need to listen to the Holy Spirit as it bridles your tongue.

All of this will take practice, practice, and more practice yet you will receive spiritual blessings along the way, and you will be a spiritual blessing to others. This is what it means to **be the Light of Christ**. You will shine as a light that others will wonder, "Where does that come from?" When they ask, because they are drawn to it, you let them know from where, Jesus Christ who Delivered you from darkness into it.

**Living the Joy of the Holy Spirit** in you is now alive. As you walk as this Light, you will become fully aware and recognize more quickly, the one voice who wants to take it away from you. Yet, he soon realizes by your stature, that he doesn't stand a chance with this fully armed "In Christ" person!

Read Ephesians 6:10-18 so that Scripture will lock in what I just shared with you. These things come from someone greater than me.

Many people often ask me, "What does it mean to live a life "Delivered" from addiction?" The answer is far from complicated, and much simpler than anyone thinks. The answer to living a "Delivered" life is the same answer that began when I showed you how to defend yourself from the wiles of the devil:

**1. Casting out Satan and his lying voice in the Name of Jesus Christ.**

**2. Staying Grounded by Reading God's Word, Scripture.**

**3. Staying in Prayer.**

**4. Living in Christian Fellowship.**

**5. Guarding my eyes, ears, hands, and mouth from the trappings of the secular world.**

**6. Walk emitting the Light of Christ.**

**7. Living the Joy of the Holy Spirit.**

Notice that I didn't say you must constantly attend addiction meetings, call yourself an addict, take a miracle pill that claims sobriety as the cure, or torture yourself daily fighting with cravings. NO! Living empowered by those 7 things for your life, is **living a life Delivered**.

Is there work ahead for you? Yes. Is it possible for you to do the work? Yes, as "I can do all things through Christ who strengthens me." (Philippians 4:13). Is there great reward along the way? For sure!

At this point in your 30-day program, I'd like you to make a Weekly schedule of when you'll be utilizing Scripture Reading, Prayer, and Fellowship in your daily routines. Planning is a major component toward the success in you living delivered. Begin your plan with the title,

"Living Delivered."

Monday:_____

_____

Tuesday:_____

_____

Wednesday: _____

_____

Thursday:_____

_____

Friday: _____

_____

Saturday: _____

_____

Sunday: _____

_____

Way to go! I encourage you to continue this into an actual calendar.

2. On page 250, a very prophetic statement is made saying, "The biggest story for you is not my story. It is what YOU have been discovering about yourself while reading it."

Many of us are uniquely different and came to be engaged in this 30-day program for a variety of personal reasons and stories. These are your personal reasons as to why and how you reached this point in your life. However, it came about, you have searched for and now found, "The Antidote for Addiction." This is the very life changing antidote that has delivered you from your addictions. In that search, you have discovered many things about yourself over the last 27 days.

Pause and take a moment to really reflect. Write down three things that you have personally discovered about yourself while taking this program.

1._____
_____
_____

2._____
_____
_____

3._____
_____
_____

Hold fast to these. Add to them when they appear to you. Look back on them if you have cause to doubt your journey. (Then renounce that thought by kicking Satan and his lie to the curb in Jesus Christ's Name.)

3. I speak further of my journey on page 251 saying, "Yet the solution to my problems came to me in the form of a different prescription, a different diagnosis. In the form of a 'Forgiveness Letter.' By studying it and learning the 'why to' and the 'how to' of forgiveness, all the puzzle pieces to my happiness began to fit together. In *forgiveness* I found a way to free myself from my past and all the negativity I'd harbored towards myself and others."

"The Antidote for Addiction," also known as "Spiritually Graced Forgiveness," has now been utilized in Your Life, on Your Journey!

How Amazing! The resentment you have carried towards that person (the pre-delivered you) has now been given to God. No longer is this your burden, but His, and rest assured, He can handle it.

I'm sure there are a few more people in your life you'd like to have receive forgiveness. It is important to be release from them as soon as possible in order to grow in your deliverance. Go back to those on your list and add any more that have come to mind since then. Then, utilizing the steps that Gary had outlined for you, and which you've already applied once. Begin again to write new "Letters of Forgiveness" for each one. Take your time with this step, and if it takes you a couple weeks, that's fine. In fact, there will be times throughout your life when you will be doing this very same thing with others again. Challenges that create areas where forgiveness is necessary are simply part of life. Isn't it wonderful that you are now armed to immediately address them and not have them put a stronghold on you.

<u>Use your journal or separate letter paper for this exercise.</u>

4. Continuing on page 253 I add,

"In writing this book I have hoped to make it possible for each and every reader to see how I was able to overcome my doubt and fear. How to gain power and control over that negative voice that spoke of them in my ear and in my mind. Grabbing ahold of my own 'will power' and saying, 'screw it' and jumping through the hoop was certainly a big part of it. But I discovered that a bigger part in conquering lies of doubt and fear was through the discovery of, and the decision in 'forgiveness.'"

My favorite word in the above passage from the book, is the word "Hoped." I find that "Hope" is a beautiful thing, especially when we find ourselves in situations of despair. The Bible tells us in Romans 5:5 that, "…hope does not disappoint, because the love of God has been poured out in our hearts by the Holy Spirit who was given to us." I encourage you to remember, that as long as you have placed your faith in Jesus Christ as your Lord and Savior, all trials and tribulations that we endure, produce hope. How wonderful! Simply put, when you go through hard times, Jesus Christ allows us to see the light at the end of the tunnel and understand that it will soon end. This is the appearance of hope in your mind, body, and spirit. He will mold you and refine you, exactly how He wants you to be. And the good news is that the trials and tribulations won't last forever. Whatever you're going through, it will have an end to its season. Yours too will reach an end!

Let's have some fun with this next exercise. Write a poem regarding Hope. It can be as long or short as you want it to be. You don't have to be a poet, anyone can do a little rhyming, right? Then, when it is completed, be bold and post your poem onto the "Antidote For Addiction" Facebook Group. If you're incarcerated while taking this program, then place your poem inside of your footlocker where you can see it daily and be reminded of this program where you grew so much in seeing it through! Or be bold and post it on the bulletin board! Are you ready? Begin.

_____

_____

_____

_____

(I didn't know you were a 'Distinguished Poet')

5. On page 254 I remember saying, "I embarked on this journey originally worrying if it would 'fail' or 'succeed.' I knew that the statistics for a successful book was not on my side as a first-time author, let alone a prisoner. Up until the point when I discovered the Power of Forgiveness, negative statistics like that consumed me. The fear of failing was great. After discovering forgiveness, those negative thoughts no longer reverberated through my mind. Eventually, I began to tell myself that the book's success based on sales was an inaccurate indicator of its success. My mind went to success being defined by "If only one person who reads my book is able to discover what I discovered and go on to have a fulfilling joyful life free of addiction, then the book would be a 100% success!"

Definitions of success seem to vary quite a bit. Before I was delivered from my addictions, and before I built the relationship with Jesus that I currently have, I thought success was to be something more worldly, more tangible. Now delivered, I find that every single day that I wake up and am able to worship God, spread the message of forgiveness through Jesus, and help those suffering from addiction, is my definition of success. Can I be successful from prison? Yes! It doesn't matter where you are physically because the real prison we were all in, prior to deliverance, was the prison of our mind, body, and spirit void of Jesus Christ. Now, operating as a new person "In Christ," freed from that prison, God irons out the other assorted details.

In a sentence or two, write your own personal definition of success.

_____
_____
_____
_____

6. I share on page 256 saying, "First using the power that comes to you when you recognize your new position as a "10" makes it possible for you to "will" changes for your life into existence. Mastering it to create your future has endless possibilities. Believe me, it can be done. I wanted to put it to the test by activating it with some of my family and friends. In my quest, I was first 'compelled' to ask my Mom to come see me, instead of continuing to wait painfully for her to find the perfect time. I knew the power of what I was using was immense but only when I actually heard my name over the prison's loudspeaker, 'Cody Lanus report to visitation,' did I truly understand its capacity to begin moving events."

Looking back, I realize now that the power that came from recognizing I was a '10' and the ability to 'will' changes for my life was from God and not from me. It was the fact that He was behind that '10' which gave me the strength of 'will' to do things that I had previously felt powerless to do. The example being reaching out to my Mom.

Now, with your recognition of Who is behind you as a '10', let's take your newfound 'will', and put your new position "In Christ" into action, just as I did. Recognizing your worth to God through Jesus Christ allows you to overcome the negative thoughts you once told yourself and allows you to accomplish things you never thought possible. Yes, you ARE delivered from addiction. Yes, you CAN now use that position "In Christ" to break down other barriers in your life that Satan once controlled.

Let's get to work. I'd like you to do something you always hesitated to do, simply because you always told yourself you weren't "worthy" or "good enough" or "capable." This can be anything you've neglected but always wanted to do. It can be someone you've been scared to communicate with but always wanted to call or write. It can be a hobby you've always wanted to try. Perhaps a diet or exercise plan you always wanted to start.

Now, embrace the fact that as a Child of God through Jesus Christ you are MORE than "worthy," you are "good enough" and you are "capable." With a Prayer and His Embrace, let today be the day you begin moving forward on that one thing you've always wanted to do, which is…

_____
_____
_____
_____
_____

Write out how you plan to implement this movement.

_____
_____
_____
_____

Finally, by God, go do it! Come back and write your date of completion and how you feel!

_____

_____
_____
_____

What a "New Person" you are! I am so proud of you. Get ready for Gary to share some things to have this journey you are on grow into a full Life Journey. Read the Afterword and I will see you on Day 28.

# DAY 28

## AFTERWARD

You have arrived at Day 28 where you will be locking in many of the things, I have encouraged you to do over the last twenty-seven days. This is where Gary relates his story of Deliverance. This is where he lays out and encourages you to take "In Christ" actions for your life. The hope is to have your own current state "of Deliverance" come alive and your future living "in Deliverance" become a believable expectation for you. Take your time with this Day. It will be a lot of work, but you are ready.

Begin with your new daily affirmation thanksgiving prayer:

*"Dear Lord, I enter this prayer in the name of Your son Jesus Christ. I pray and thank You for allowing my faith in You to come alive in me as I continue through this 30-day program. I know that it is by faith that I continue forward, as I'm seeking something that sometimes feels impossible to conquer. By trusting You, I know that anything is possible including faith in being delivered from drugs and alcohol. Your word says, "For by Grace you have been saved through faith." Father, I believe that by my faith in You, I am Delivered. In Jesus Christ's name, Amen."*

Be sure to re-read the Afterword and remember this will be Gary's (The Old Man) voice speaking to you. He is now the "I" that is sharing.

## THE OLD MAN'S WORDS OF ENCOURAGEMENT

1. "I will remember the words of the Lord, Surely, I will remember Your wonders of old." Psalm 77:11

I share with you on pages 262 and 263 saying,

"Crying and shaking I put my hands up in the air toward the ceiling and said, 'Dear God I cannot do this anymore. This is so much bigger than I am, or ever will be. Please, please, please take it from me. Forgive me for being such a fool. Please!"

Having reached this far into "Your 30-Day Deliverance Program" and recognizing and receiving the "Antidote For Addiction," I have great hope that you have already had your personal moment of recognition and the words that produced them, as I did that early morning in 2001. You have already been called by Cody to write different versions of this throughout your program as your own life was revisited before your very eyes. I believe "Living Delivered" begins and is grounded in the remembrance of that very moment(s) it happened for you. I believe this will come to be known as one of your Greatest Spiritual Markers (A life changing wonderful event so powerful and impactful that you know, without question, that its reality could have only come upon you from God). This is a "moment in time" life landmark that will not be moved. This Great Spiritual Marker is the place where you will return to, remembering where Christ defeated the lie for you, and revealed the truth of your "Deliverance!"

Therefore, I encourage you to take this time to get clear on when that was, what it looked like, what it sounded like, what it felt like and write it out in full. In doing so, it will become so deeply imbedded into your heart, soul, strength, mind, and spirit you will be able to "stand" on it when needed. Standing firm when the unhealthy, unholy voice tries to knock you off your mark! Cody has done a wonderful job letting you be aware of this voice, her voice, his old "she" voice, the one you once believed as truth, and how to expose it as a lie, to be renounced.

Now, pause and take a moment to write it out thus preparing yourself for when "she" attempts to creep back in!

What did your Spiritual Marker moment look, sound, and feel like?

_____
_____
_____
_____
_____
_____
_____
_____
_____

2. I continue on page 264 saying,

"As a confirmation that today really was the day that drinking would be behind me."

I spoke of Spiritual Markers above and their importance to you. Now, the many "Confirmations" that have and will come in your deliverance from addiction should also be noted and remembered by you as well. (Confirmations are specific unfolding events that lend great credence to the reality of your Spiritual Markers.) My "Confirmations" began very early that morning when my Mom used the words, "That 'will' be nice." The reason it jumped out at me and caught my ear was that it was different from what she had said, as well as everyone else negatively affected by my addiction had said when I would promise them, "Never Again!" They all had previously said, "That 'would' be nice." Yet, this time she said, "That 'will' be nice." The use of "will" instead of "would" was special. For the first time it felt like someone else was speaking of "belief in me," not just "hope for me." That just felt good. Now, the biggest reason I believed I heard something that tiny was because the Holy Spirit In me was pricking me to listen! The biggest reason I believe my Mom said it that day was because the Holy Spirit In her pricked her to know she could truly believe it, thus giving me the words of "confirmation."

Understand this my friends, the Holy Spirit works in others as mightily as He works in you when you engage Him, and He engages you (Like my Mom and I that morning). When you are obedient to what He calls you to, and you wait expectantly for the blessings that come when you call upon Him, the confirmations will come. It will take time to experience "Confirmations" for your "Spiritual Markers" as it did for and continues to for myself and Cody. But never, ever, never, ever doubt that they are there. I encourage you to continue what Cody has already been calling you to do and record the events.

Pause and begin to fill out the two sides below. Begin by listing your Great Spiritual Marker of Deliverance on the left and then on the right, writing out the Confirmation moment(s). The moments when you just knew, it had to be true. When you felt it, saw it, heard it, or spoke it!

SPIRITUAL MARKER            CONFIRMATION

_____/_____
_____/_____
_____/_____
_____/_____
_____/_____
_____/_____
_____/_____
_____/_____
_____/_____
_____/_____
_____/_____
_____/_____
_____/_____
_____/_____

Now, your life supported by Spiritual Markers and Confirmations has begun. I challenge you to use your journal and keep this going for the rest of your life. The unholy, unhealthy voice will be trying to take it away from you. But, the Shield of Faith evident in Your Spiritual Markers, Confirmed and used by you in the Name of Jesus Christ will "…quench all the fiery darts of the wicked one!" Ephesians 6:16

3. "Ask, and it will be given to you; seek, and you will find; knock, and it will be opened to you." Matthew 7:7

On page 264 I reveal more by saying, "In the days to follow when the issue arose, which with so many drinking friends happened often, I let them know the same thing I let my mother know, 'This will never happen again.' Their disbelief was understood as they had heard similar words from me for years. They did not realize there was something different going on behind those words. At the same time I couldn't really describe it, as I was still in a bit of amazement myself. Yet, over time I realized exactly what it was, God's Deliverance. And what it wasn't. It wasn't a mask, or a "live with-it" training system, or a coping method or an accepting "as is" method. It didn't have twelve steps, though it had a few. It wasn't a daily reminder of my past failings as if still lived."

It goes without saying that these types of questions, "What about my friends? What will I say to them? How am I to operate around them? Can I even be around them?" etc. were in the forefront of my mind as I stepped out into my 'Delivered Life.' They are, or will be, in the forefront of yours as well. Let me say that the biggest, best, and always most truthful and powerful answer to these questions come from God, not man. Then when you speak, they are confirming statements, not possibility statements as if you yourself still question them. The Holy Spirit in You will be bringing to your memory, mind, and mouth the things you will need to say and the positions you will need to take. You need to get good at calling upon Him and then hearing His Voice. This is done by practicing, practicing, and practicing.

Here is an example of a time when it happened to me.

I went to God on the track one day in prison so frustrated because I seemed to not be hearing an answer from God on a question that I had asked Him over and over again. A question about how to best engage a "new to prison" inmate named Ralph. My French and Irish language got the better of me that day, to the point where anyone walking near me knew for sure I couldn't be talking to God, yet I was. I asked Him "Why are You not answering me?!" He spoke right back as only God can when He said,

"Gary, I am not confused with your prayer, I know exactly what you are asking, but you are confused and therefore cannot hear my answer! You have layered your prayer about that person into so many mini prayers concerning your engagement with him, you cannot even hear My answer to the first one! Stop right now, separate your prayer into a list of yes or no questions of me at each step. Then listen and do what I say at each one! You will no longer be confused but you will be confronted with a choice, to do what I say or not. I will be right here for you when you need My Self-Control at that step!"

Many of you understand what I just said immediately, for others it will take a while to understand and break your old habits of layering prayers to the point of 'your' confusion. Then, move into creating yes/no prayers for your better understanding of His voice.

I encourage you to pause right now and take on the same task as God laid out for me that day. Utilizing the same below, taking the most important layered prayer you have gone to God with, yet not heard a clear answer. Separate it into yes/no questions. Then go to

God with each one separately. Do not move on to the next one until you hear His Voice of Direction on the first. I have provided my layered question that day as an example for you.

**LAYERED PRAYER**

"Dear God, Ralph just came into the area and seems so lost, in so many ways that he needs my help. Will You please give me the abilitymto reach out and speak to him. Let him be comfortable with opening up to me, so that I will know what areas to help him in first…etc."

**YES/NO QUESTIONS**

1. "Do You want me to go and help Ralph?"

2. "Do You want me to take my Bible with me when I see him?"

3. "Do You want me to go right to Your Saving Grace right away?"

4. "Do you want me to tell him what You first told me?"

**LAYERED PRAYER**                **YES/NO QUESTIONS**

_____      1._____
_____      2._____
_____      3._____
_____      4._____
_____      5._____

_____      1._____
_____      2._____
_____      3._____
_____      4._____
_____      5._____

| LAYERED PRAYER | YES/NO QUESTIONS |
|---|---|
| _____ | 1._____ |
| _____ | 2._____ |
| _____ | 3._____ |
| _____ | 4._____ |
| _____ | 5._____ |

You will get a chuckle out of what happened to me that day on the track and what I learned when I asked the first question, "Do you want me to go and help Ralph?" I heard almost instantly "NO!" I heard it so quickly it shocked me. I really felt as if I was still "confused." "Why would God not want me to go talk to Ralph?" So, I doubled down and tried to help with my confusion by reversing the question and said, "Ok God, does this mean you do not want me to engage Ralph?" BAM! Before I even got the last letter of Ralph's name off my lips, I heard "YES!" Wow! Seems my ego had no place in the equation that day. So, I chose to be obedient and not engage Ralph.

On that day God gave me an even bigger revelation than the one about layered prayer and Ralph. He revealed something about Himself and how He operates with us. See, if the answer to my first question was "NO!" and I was obedient to it, then the next 3+ questions I had for God would not need to be asked. They carried no weight and needed no reply! Go back and look at my example and try to understand that this same thing will also happen to you, clearing up any confusion over His Voice. This will save you a lot of time on things that you are not called to do. Trust me, you will be called to do enough, your share. God will not leave you out!

I encourage you to think hard on this situation I present. If you embrace what God gave me that day on the track as a better way to be clear, then you will become better and better, sooner, and sooner, at hearing His Voice. This is your way of asking, seeking, and knocking from Matthew 7:7. This is where you will find many doors being opened with answers to your new way of Petitioning, Questioning Prayers.

4. I open up some revelation of understanding in excerpts from pages 266 – 268 with,

"I began by recognizing my own forgiveness, then set out to model that. I believed I could not wait for people to change before I forgave them. The only way for it to be a permanent release was to give it over to the same one who took it from me, God. When I did it was instant and complete."

"Spiritually Graced Forgiveness" is the type that God used on me. I knew full well I owed a debt for all I had done. A really big debt. I knew I was struggling to find better behaviors that wouldn't continue to add to the debt I owed. Yet, right in the middle of all that, someone was willing to forgive me without me paying the debt, by allowing someone else to pay it for me. I wasn't deserving of it, but someone did it anyway, God. When someone does that physically, mentally, or spiritually it is called grace. Grace being "unmerited favor given." It is one of the rarest types of forgiveness on earth, but it is the only type that comes from God. Jesus Christ is that very Grace."

"It took me quite some time to discover that the same permanent Spiritually Graced Forgiveness was available to be used by me with others in my life. Years to make the transition from one to the other. But when I did, the full power of that Antidote for Addiction began to play out in every area of my life. God had allowed the debt of my infractions to go to Christ and be no more. I had finally realized He also allowed me to take the debt of infractions against me by others to Christ and have them be no more as well. <u>When that happened the pain of the debt disappeared.</u> This is Spiritually Graced Forgiveness. It is available to you, and for you." (added underline for emphasis)

This is where it all comes together for your future "Delivered Life." It is the mechanism by which God made it possible through His Grace, Jesus Christ, for you to live a "Delivered In Christ Life." Living this life with others from here on out, for the rest of your days. Acknowledging It has happened to you, Accepting It has happened to you, and Engaging that It has happened to you, is now yours. You're now In Christ, and the Holy Spirit lives in you.

When I acknowledged, accepted, and engaged this within myself, God gave me the vision and peace to understand something very important: He allowed me to see that just because He forgave me and delivered me from my sinful addictive self, did not mean that everyone else in my realm was going to automatically do the same. It was but for me to ask forgiveness from others, yet it was between them and God if they did or not. I was called to rest in the fact that their forgiveness of me was not in my control but His. It was for Him to deal with the timing of that forgiveness.

As you embrace this truth, He will allow His Peace, in the Fruit of His Holy Spirit in you, to rise up and give you comfort to move forward even in their unforgiveness. When this happens in your life, I encourage you to do what He called me to do. I "prayed a blessing into them" and still do, to this day, as I was called to do in 1 Peter 3:8,9. You are called to do the same. I encourage you to do so, then keep moving, and you will inherit a blessing.

"And the peace of God, which surpasses all understanding, will guard your heart and mind through Jesus Christ."

Philippians 4:7

Always remember, God's got you.

Please open your Bibles to read both of the above passages. Get familiar with them. Refer to them when you need to in the future.

My continued discussion of the workings of "forgiveness" is because I have found it to be one of the biggest challenges and stumbling blocks in living a life delivered. Satan uses this area to stop men and women in their tracks by feelings of being wounded or hurt in others unforgiveness. So, stay with me here and trust me when I say you will be glad that you did.

"And you, being dead in your trespasses and the uncircumcision of your flesh, He has made alive together with Him, having forgiven you all trespasses, having wiped out the handwriting of requirements that was against us, which was contrary to us. And He has taken it out of the way, having nailed it to the cross. Having disarmed the principalities and powers, He made a public spectacle of them, triumphing over them in it." Colossians 2:13-15

Cody had you write out some forgiveness letters. He has also shown you that the power of the letters is not in their delivery or acceptance, it is in the fact that you opened your heart to offer forgiveness and to seek forgiveness. I am proud of you for digging in with Faith on these letters and the letters that have yet to be spoken or written. You are on the right path for living Delivered as you use them whenever needed. I underlined "***When that happened the pain of the debt disappeared***" in the above section to draw your attention to the fact that you can receive and live out this "release of debt" in your life of forgiveness.

Grab your Bible and read for yourself Colossians 2:13-15. Read it three times. Though you can readily see yourself in 2:13,14, I want you to really focus on 2:15, "Having **disarmed the principalities and powers**, He made a public spectacle of them, triumphing over them in it."

Can you see how this makes it possible for you to live free from the previous **pain "caused" by your sin** against God? Hold on to that realization as you continue.

It doesn't take us long to recognize that the **pain** of someone's transgressions against us, is what eats us alive. The **pain** we feel from the transgression becomes so strong; we demand a debt be paid for it. This is why "Intellectually Reasoned Forgiveness" is never a forever forgiveness. Yes, the thought of the action is gone, out of sight out of mind, but the **pain** 'caused' by the action remains underneath, buried somewhere deep inside you. It is waiting to spring out again at the very first hint of another transgression by the same person, and it most often does.

Thankfully, what you have now experienced, and have available in every forgiveness scenario of your life, is the type of "Spiritually Graced Forgiveness" spoken of in Colossians 2:13-15. That is the type of forgiveness where ***the pain "caused" by the debt disap-***

***pears.*** It literally does not exist in you to recall. It is gone from you. Where did it go!? You nailed it to the Cross of Christ! When you did this, "He disarmed the principalities and powers of it," the very *pain* "caused" by the debt is no longer yours but God's through Jesus Christ.

Pause and reach back to take one of the forgiveness scenarios you have worked through with Cody's guidance and re-forgive it within the context of Colossians 2:13-15. Speak the prayerful words that give the person, the transgression, and the pain of it, to the Cross of Christ. Thank God for allowing you to forgive your transgressor just as God forgave you through Jesus Christ.

Write out below in your own words what you experienced in doing this, including any feelings that came about. (Peace, Release, Ease, Freedom, etc.)

_____
_____
_____
_____
_____
_____
_____

Continue as you move forward in your life recording the moments of 'Spiritually Graced Forgiveness' as they come about. Hold any future transgressions of others to this tenet of your Christian Faith. By doing so, you will come to know for sure if you have only offered someone 'Intellectually Reasoned Forgiveness' or genuinely offered 'Spiritually Graced Forgiveness.

This will take as much practice, practice, practice as anything Cody has called you to. Let God build in you a lifetime of releases to Him.

5. I speak of you openly on page 269 saying,

"You have now joined Cody on his journey of the same discovery. You have felt his pain and had pain of your own arise as you have traveled. You have been able to witness how he has navigated the things that popped up along the way of which some were even of his own making. You have seen how he once resisted and hesitated to even look at it, then go on to face it, encounter it, embrace it, and receive it, the Antidote for Addiction, forgiveness. He has laid all this before you in the snapshot of his life. You recognize that he is still on the journey as I was after my own discovery. This is a wonderful thing. This is the way it's supposed to be. My hope for you is in all that you have read, you recognize the most important thing of all, you, and your relationship with God! That you recognize as you reach the end of this book you are in actuality reaching the end of the new Chapter 1 of your own story. The story of what has happened to you physically, emotionally, and spiritually while on this journey is your Chapter 2."

By the very fact that you are right here, right now shows that you have been building on from your Chapter 2 into many more Chapters of your life. What a journey you have been Called to be on. Yes, I believe that it is God Himself who has pricked you in the Spirit to be Called to Deliverance. You have been obedient to that call and done what you have been called to do to arrive. Your life in retrospect, and in the future, is made up of many Chapters. Our hope is that in remembering this, you will be better equipped to recall all of your Spiritual Markers that God lays before you. You will start to build a bank of Spiritual Markers to fall back on. I encourage you to find those that you can return to in the future. During the times when that voice of doubt creeps in and tries to debilitate you, making it seem impossible to move forward or believe in yourself enough to do so. The times when you stop and say,

*"In the name of Jesus Christ, Satan and your lying voice be gone from me now. In the name of Jesus Christ, I cast you and your voice back down under Christ's feet where you belong. Dear God let your Holy Spirit Voice of Truth fill the space that was just left when I cast Satan and his voice out in Your Son's Name. I believe in Your belief in me to move now. Thank You in Jesus' Name. Amen"*

Every time I have prayed that prayer, I have had one of my Spiritual Markers, where God had delivered me before, come to mind. It was a time back in 2012 when I literally fell to my knees in front of my couch and said a form of that prayer. It was when the ceiling and walls of my life began to crush in on me, with the revelation that "my gig" was up and I was to be exposed for all that I had been doing. In that instant, God reached down from my "prayer for mercy" with this,

"I've got you! Get up, what lies ahead will be long and difficult, but I will see you through it!"

Had I not heard it, or had I not believed it, or had I not acted on it, you most likely would not be reading these very words I type almost 10 years later. It was that very Spiritual Marker that I turned to again and again in prison and well beyond. It still comes to me today at the most appropriate time for my life, reminding me of God's Mercy.

My friend, you are now living that for yourself. You are building your Spiritual Markers. I have great faith in you to stay that course for your life. To live the "Delivered Life" that God has called you to live.

Always remember that you have already proven that you have the ability, "In Christ," to cast that un-holy, un-healthy spirit, Satan, in all his forms and voices out and free up room for the Holy Spirit Voice of God to be heard.

Furthermore, you have the ability and confidence to hear the Healthy Voice of Reason from God. Reach up, and reach out, there is a myriad of doors waiting to be opened just for you. It all begins right now with your belief in God's belief in you. There is nothing Greater. You are, always were, and will remain "The Rose!" Stand in that truth and take the next steps Cody has put before you. Soon you will grow into that belief in yourself.

May you continue to live in the Peace God has placed before you. Take

actions for the abundant Peace of your Life you seek, forgiven, freed and delivered of addiction by the true Antidote for Addiction, Spiritually Graced Forgiveness.

May God's Peace abound in your life. He believes in you for just that!

# DAY 29

## CONGRATULATIONS!

Welcome to Day 29, your next to the last day of this 30-Day To Life Journey. Let's celebrate by deeply expressing this 29th Day Prayer of Thanksgiving:

*"Dear Lord, I enter this prayer in the name of Your Son Jesus Christ. I pray and thank You for allowing my faith in You to continue to come alive in me as I near the conclusion of this 30-Day Journey. I know that it is by faith that I have come to this day and by faith that I continue forward, growing in learning Your Ways to 'Live Delivered.' By trusting You, I know that anything is possible, including faith in my "In Christ" deliverance from drugs and alcohol. Your word says, "For by Grace you have been saved through faith." Father, I believe that by my faith in You, I will live out my life, Delivered. In Jesus Christ's name, Amen.*

As page 271 says,

"CONGRATULATIONS!"
"Way to Go!"
"You made it on your journey with Cody through
*Surviving The Perfect Storm Of Addiction.*"
"Don't Stop Now!
Don't Turn Back!"

Well, you sure took that Congratulations from the end of the TATTOOS book to heart. You didn't stop. You didn't turn back. In fact, you made the decision to take action, real action by embracing and engaging the 30-Day to Life Deliverance Program.

This Program was designed to allow you to see the Who, What, When, Where, Why, and How of Cody and Gary's Deliverance from Alcohol and Addiction. This, with the hope that you might embrace and engage the same into your personal experience of Deliverance. Then, continuing to grow in it, and live out your full Life of Deliverance.

You and the Good Lord know exactly where you were when you started your 30-Day to Life Deliverance Program and exactly where you are today. Our hope is that you find yourself *in Christ delivered* and ready to embrace the "What Next?" for your life.

We are calling upon you to complete one last task. When it is done there will be waiting for you a wonderful "Certificate of Completion" of the Antidote For Addiction's 30-Day To Life Deliverance Program.

Ok, here it is. Take a few minutes and think back on where you were prior to entering the Program. Let your mind drift through the days that you worked so hard, sometimes with great struggle, yet persevered. Then, land on where you are today, right here, right now. Now, use the space below to write out in your own words what your experience has been.

Ready, begin.

## MY 30-DAY JOURNEY

_____
_____
_____
_____
_____
_____
_____
_____
_____

Nice job my friend!

Though we would love to see your words, or even have you post them on the Antidote for Addiction Group Page, that is not a requirement for this exercise. If you choose to share that is up to you.

The most important piece of this exercise is in you seeing what you have experienced and expressed in words. In you believing it. In you, knowing it to be your 30-Day Journey "In Christ." Something no one can take away from you.

All you need to do is write, email, text, call, or post with your name and the words "Day 29 Complete." Then your well-earned Certificate will be on its way for you to frame and put out for your family, friends and loved ones to see. Then again, everyone at Antidote For Addiction would love to have you take a photo of you holding your Certificate and post it to the Group. We look forward to hearing of your completion.

Please know that we are and will remain very proud of you for all you have committed to God and yourself within this Program. We both know what goes into arriving where you find yourself now.

"Way to Go!" is in order once again.

Before we end this day, Cody has put together a wonderful prayer for you. Say it now and know that there are others right there with you in the Spirit of Christ.

*"Dear God, I thank You for the freedom in my deliverance from addiction. For allowing me to no longer see or have the need to label myself as an addict. I thank You for Your Strength in me to complete this 30-day to Life Program. Father, I know that my New Direction forward will be a direction filled with Your blessings, and that although I may stumble in other areas from time to time, as a Child of Yours I will never fail as I remain in my position "In Christ." I thank You for my health and safety in making it this far. Thank You for your continued guidance and protection over my life and the life of my loved ones. Thank You for not allowing Satan to prevail over my addiction, for it was You Father who prevailed through Your Son, Jesus Christ on the cross at Calvary. Thank You for allowing me to prevail by the same Cross of Christ. In the precious name of Jesus Christ, I thank You for Your Deliverance Power, Amen!"*

Now, rest on this today and we will see you on Day 30 to answer the question, "What Next?"

Congratulations from both of us,

Cody Lanus and Gary Martel

# DAY 30

## WHAT'S NEXT?

### MOVING FROM CODY'S STORY TO YOUR STORY NOW INTO YOUR LIFE!

By arriving right here, right now at the 30th day of this Powerful Program of Deliverance is living proof that you did exactly what you were called to do at the end of the TATTOOS book, page 271 where it reads,

"Let Your Chapter #2 begin right here, right now. Whether you are one who is, like Cody & Gary once were, personally caught up in the throes of Addiction or if you are one that has taken this journey in order to better understand the face of addiction and help a loved one, we encourage you to take the next step…Pray…

…and right then or at some time thereafter you prayed,

"Dear God, Thank You for having me read and witness Your Spiritually Graced Forgiveness, completing the first Chapter of my own journey to deliverance and freedom. I am asking You, right here right now for this very forgiveness over me (over the life of my loved one) who suffers from the un-holy, un-healthy voice of addiction. May you reveal to me the Grace from which this comes. May you open my heart to hear Your Voice that I may Trust in You to be positioned In You to receive Your deliverance. I am ready. In Jesus Name, Amen,"

Then you chose to take the further step and click on or reach out to "My Chapter #2" at AntidoteforAddition.com to engage this 30-Day To Life Deliverance Program.

Wow! What an amazing journey of Deliverance you have been on. One Guided by the Holy Spirit of God in you. Congratulations once again.

Your certificate is on its way to you. Be proud of yourself for achieving such a monumental goal by allowing yourself to come under the Guidance of the Good Lord, by having an "Encounter of the Heart" with Jesus Christ.

I am sure that "What's Next?" is a question that is looming somewhere in your mind. Our hope is to answer it in such a way that you will not become overwhelmed by engaging your new "In Christ" Delivered life with family, friends, loved ones, co-workers, associates, fellow Christians, and the like.

**First**, acknowledge, accept, and engage the fact that you are never alone, even when you feel you are. The Holy Spirit of God is always with you and is but a conversation away. Never fail to open up your voice for His direction. Always and in Everything. You will get some good practice in this especially with what I am about to say:

**Second**, Satan has put his devils, demons, minions, fiends, and imps on notice that there is a new person (you) "In Christ" that Satan has lost to the Deliverance of Addiction. They are called to be ready to try and work directly in you, or indirectly through other's voices and actions, to convince you to let it go, stop believing it and come back. These will be "lies" of the highest order. The sooner you accept this, recognize them, and cast them out, the better for you, and the less often he will try again. Live in the light of victory and use that light to cast out the dark when it tries to enter. This is not to scare you, or have you cowered in fear but to inform you that it exists, is coming, and for you to be readily aware. You are already armed as evident in the fact that:

**Third**, you have been given the power to cast out Satan in all his forms and language (voice) in the Name of Jesus Christ. Use Jesus Christ's name as often as you need to "send packing" the unholy spirit of Satan and all his forms. Bookmark your program at Day 28 on the page where your "Casting Out" prayer was used. Memorize this prayer until you own it without having to even think first. Then you will find yourself redirecting Satan before he even gets a word or two in. Practice, Practice, Practice! Satan hates you doing this; therefore, you should love it!

**Fourth**, you will grow in your Delivered Life proportionally with your growth in your personal Christian Fellowship. You learned about the power of this in the Program. Now that you are morphing out from the cocoon of the actual 30-day program into Life, it is important to surround yourself with fellow Christians. You were asked earlier in the program to pray about and seek out a new Church or renew your relationship with a previous one to begin this very Fellowship. To let someone in the ministry know that you were going through a "Spiritually Graced Forgiveness" Addiction Deliverance Program. This was to have someone in the Fellowship praying for you as well as someone that you can go to upon completion. We encourage you to pray with that fellowship minister as to God's calling for you. Our prayer is that you take on some role within the body of the Church.

You are now a wonderful example of God's Grace and the light you shine should be welcome in that community of fellow Christians. Be patient but be as creative as the Holy Spirit calls you to be. Then be obedient to the call you hear.

If you had not done this during the Program, it is imperative that you do it now. God has great faith in you to do just that. Let your light shine.

He may call you to be the one who leads another into the Antidote for Addiction system, where God, found in the Book and Program, will lead them to Deliverance. What a blessing that will be.

**Fifth**, continue growing your relationship with God. This is a lifelong process and a beautiful one at that. He is always at work around you and available for you to engage Him. You actually put together in the Program one or two weekly schedules laying out how you would incorporate this into your days. Refer to it often and let it be your guide to creating a full-time calendar for your life. Remember the four ways or places that God Speaks. Be sure your calendar is habitually full of showing up where His voice is heard. Here is a reminder.

1. **Scripture (Daily in the Word)**

2. **Witness of other Christians (Fellowship, music, books, sermons)**

3. **Circumstances (Godscidences/Providentially Perfectly Timed Events)**

4. **Prayer (conversational, worship, praise, petition, thanksgiving)**

The greatest way to grow your experience with God is through obedience to His call. Yet, unless you show up in ALL these 4 places where He does His calling you will find it hard to Obey His Voice.

**Sixth,** at your earliest possible moment go to www.antidoteforaddiction.com and enter your email address.

Join the **"Antidote For Addiction"** Facebook Group by clicking on the Group Button, **"AFA Facebook Group"**

- You are highly encouraged to become part of this group as a valuable, continually growing resource for your delivered life. If you choose not to engage right away that is fine. Yet, go there as often as possible to read what other like-minded "In Christ" Delivered Christians are sharing. Become a vacuum for learning from others. This is part of the Fellowship. When you are ready, you can jump in and engage.

Then, click on **"What's Next Resources"** where, as a Certified AFA Graduate, you will find a number of helpful tools for living your delivered life. Navigate your way to the things that will resonate best to where you find yourself in your Delivered Life Journey. Return often to receive any new resources as they become available.

Finally, remember you are never alone "In Christ" and in fellowship with Antidote For Addiction. You may choose to provide your questions within the Facebook Group where they will be fielded, answered, or redirected to the best source. Yet, if you ever need to reach out for a more personal setting be sure to add into your email list gary@antidoteforaddiction.com and send along your questions where we will field them, answer them, or redirect them to the best source for you to receive guidance. **IF A HOTLINE IS NEEDED CALL 919-244-9770**

- If you are restricted in your access to the Internet or to Facebook, we still want you to be connected and have all possible resources available. In order to do this please write, email, text, or call in your contact information to:

    Antidote For Addiction
    288 Deerfield Estates Rd.
    Boone, NC 28607
    984-227-2729

    We will send along instructions on how to obtain the available resources. Our prayer is you reach out to us for support.

Here is a word about the "Four Pillars" for your Delivered Life from Cody Lanus, the Author and Creator, the man who loves you, cares about you, prays for you, and has lived exactly where you are right now. Trust that his words matter.

"So, what will your new life look like?"

"What should you expect as someone delivered from addiction? The short answer is that you should expect Love, God's Love. Embracing that Love and allowing the flame within you to grow will happen all on its own "with obedience" to The Holy Spirit, so be patient. You now have this Great Power within you. However, you must not be ignorant of Satan's devices and continue to sharpen your skills with this new power that now dwells inside of you. So maybe the question shouldn't be "What's Next" but rather "What NOW"?

1. **Direction**: Continue steadfast in **prayer**. Developing a good prayer life is key to allowing the Holy Spirit to speak in you and through you.

2. **Connection**: You don't need a meeting or a 12-step program, you need **fellowship.** Find a good Bible based, Holy Spirit filled church near you. Get into a good routine of attending and even participating in different Church led activities and ministries. The connection and fellowship will help you grow and flourish even further.

3. **Protection**: Protect yourself from the snares of Satan by continuing to **read the Word**. Get into a good reading schedule. It can be 10 minutes a day if that's all you have, the key is to simply start. The first step is always the hardest. Always remember that God is right there with you every single step of the way.

4. **Antidote for Addiction**: Finally, applying "**Spiritually Graced Forgiveness**" by utilizing the steps that are outlined in "Tattoos, My Gateway Drug" and "The 30-Day To Life Program" are essential to living your life Delivered. Reapplying the steps to those we've forgiven or applying them to people we may need to forgive in the future, is what is needed, whenever Satan attempts to rear his ugly head and sow seeds of resentment in your life. You "NOW" have the tool to remain in your Delivered position "In

Christ," "Spiritually Graced Forgiveness!" Never forget that the ability to apply those steps is now in your hand.

I am confident that if you make these four pillars of your delivered life, Christian Faith a part of your regular schedule, the Holy Spirit within you will speak louder and clearer day by day. Will you encounter temptation in your life again? Sure. I would be naive to think those situations will be eliminated completely. I myself often encounter temptation. However, I "Thank God" for my delivered position and for "Spiritually Graced Forgiveness." Whenever I encounter situations of temptation I,

1. Recognize my position "In Christ."

2. Listen to the Holy Spirit within me telling me very clear instructions on what to do and what not to do.

3. Make a "Delivered Decision."

It's no more complicated than that. Honestly, the more situations you encounter, the easier it gets. Not the other way around. Yes, we live in very challenging times that make it difficult for an addict. However, there is good news, "YOU ARE NO LONGER AN ADDICT, YOU ARE DELIVERED!" Praise God!"

## A LETTER OF THANKS

We would like to take the time to thank you for your participation in and your completion of the "30-Day To Life, Deliverance Program." We hope you know your importance as a child of God and hold true to that position "In Christ" through your continued obedience of His Voice. It is He who let you know that you are not an "addict."

A "meeting" or "12 steps" to continually remain sober are not necessary as YOU NOW HAVE THE MOST POWERFUL ENERGY SOURCE IN THE UNIVERSE WITHIN YOU, THE HOLY SPIRIT! This is the same Real Power Source you now call on daily for strength, guidance, and comfort, as your Helper.

We are proud of you and all you've accomplished through the engagement of the Book and Program.

We know it has been challenging, yet you have endured.

We know that your future is bright and filled with many of God's blessings as you continue to call on Him for patience, strength, wisdom, and direction.

May God bless you in all you do "In Christ."

Your Fellow Delivered Friends,

Cody Lanus & Gary Martel

# ADDITONAL NOTES

# ADDITIONAL NOTES

# ADDITIONAL NOTES

# ADDITIONAL NOTES

# ADDITIONAL NOTES

## ABOUT THE AUTHOR/CREATOR

Cody Lanus is an Iowa native, raised in Omaha Nebraska, and moved on to attend High School and College in the Kansas City, Missouri area. He worked hard mentally and physically, rising to become a Star Athlete in multiple sports with his Highest Achievements in High School and College Football. Many who were in the stands will still remember his name today. The powerful, compelling, and moving story of his descent from that high position into a world of drugs, and how he "Survived the Perfect Storm of Addiction" were written within the pages of TATTOOS, My Gateway Drug.

He has now followed up that story with this "highly personalized" 30 Days To Life Deliverance Program. His hope and prayer are by opening up the steps of his journey, he may help you or a loved one embrace, engage, and experience "Deliverance" from the throes of Addiction.

Cody is currently sharing this very program to his fellow inmates, while he is serving out the remainder of a 12-year prison sentence. This is where he was able to find his "True Self" and "Discover" what it takes to walk out of that destructive "Perfect Storm," Delivered.

# ABOUT THE COLLABORATOR

Gary Martel was "called" to turn his six-year experience as a "white-collar" prisoner, and the revelations of the deep study into the core forces within himself that led him there, into the PriscillAquila Enterprise. He is now the founder, grantor, and facilitator of this Christian "Business Missions" Development Company. He is the Host of Seminars, Webinars, Workshops, and Mastermind Groups made available through the PriscillAquila Institute, the Training and Resource division. He also hosts the weekly PriscillAquila Power Podcasts covering an array of topics that impact Christian "Business Missions" Entrepreneurs, Employees, and Ministries.

Gary collaborated with Cody Lanus in writing and publishing TATTOOS, My Gateway Drug, Surviving The Perfect Storm Of Addiction in 2021. He has continued to work with Cody in bringing to the world the follow-up Antidote for Addiction "30 Days To Life Deliverance Program" which you now have at your hand.

Gary is also the author of two creative non-fiction manuscripts, "Thirty Years in the Wilderness" and "Fifty Years A Thief" which are currently in the pre-publication phase with the PriscillAquila Press.

# BIBLIOGRAPHY

The Holy Bible, New King James Version, Thomas Nelson Inc. 1982

Greg Bishop, The Logan Effect, Sports Illustrated, March 11, 2019, page 66.

Tupac Shakur, Hail Mary, Universal Music Corporation, February 11, 1997

# ADDITIONAL RESOURCES

**BUILDING YOUR RELATIONSHIP WITH GOD:**

Henry Blackaby, *Experiencing God / Knowing and Doing the Will of God*, B&H Publishing Group, 2008, 2021

**LIVING LIFE DELIVERED:**

Joseph Saladino, *You're Invited: To Discover A Predictable Path To Peace, Joy, and Freedom*, Healing for the Heart Ministries, 2019

Clay Waters, *The Ripple Effect / The 7 Most Important Decisions of Each Day* / WestBow Press, 2012

Bob Record / Randy Singer, *Made To Count / Discovering What To Do With Your Life*, W Publishing Group, a Division of Thomas Nelson, 2002

www.ingramcontent.com/pod-product-compliance
Lightning Source LLC
Chambersburg PA
CBHW072148100526
44589CB00015B/2142